RELATIVE VALUES

A Light Comedy

by

NOËL COWARD

SAMUEL

FRENCH

LONDON

NEW YORK TORONTO SYDNEY HOLLYWOOD

ISBN 0 573 01375 6

RELATIVE VALUES

Presented by H. M. Tennent Ltd. and John C. Wilson at the Savoy Theatre, London, on 28th November 1951, with the following cast of characters:

(*in the order of their appearance*)

CRESTWELL, the butler	*Richard Leech*
ALICE, the housemaid	*Renee Hill*
MRS DORA MOXTON (MOXIE)	*Angela Baddeley*
FELICITY, Countess of Marshwood	*Gladys Cooper*
LADY CYNTHIA HAYLING	*Dorothy Batley*
THE HONOURABLE PETER INGLETON, Felicity's nephew	*Simon Lack*
ADMIRAL SIR JOHN HAYLING	*Charles Cullum*
NIGEL, Earl of Marshwood	*Ralph Michael*
MIRANDA FRAYLE	*Judy Campbell*
DON LUCAS	*Hugh McDermott*

The play directed by the Author

SYNOPSIS OF SCENES

The action of the play passes in the library of Marshwood House, East Kent, during early July 1951

ACT I

SCENE 1 Saturday afternoon

SCENE 2 Two hours later

ACT II

SCENE 1 Before dinner

SCENE 2 After dinner

ACT III

The following morning

Photograph by Angus McBean

ACT I*

Scene 1

SCENE—*The library of Marshwood House, East Kent. A Saturday afternoon early in July 1951.*

The most important feature of the library of Marshwood House, is that it is not a library. It may have been in the past and it may be in the future, but now it is quite definitely the family living-room. There are double doors up R *opening into the hall. A door down* R *leads to the study. The fireplace is* C *of the wall* R. *There is a pillared alcove* L *with french windows leading on to a paved terrace with the garden beyond, which, like most Kentish gardens, is inwardly sure of itself but outwardly rather confused. There are wooded hills in the distance and the sea is not far away. The room is furnished comfortably and charmingly but without any particular design. The chintz covers are old and a little faded and all the furniture, which is of mixed periods, gives the impression that it has drifted into the room at one time or another, taken a liking to it, and decided to settle down. Below the door down* R *there is an ornate games table. Above the door there is a comfortable deep red plush tub chair. The fireplace has a heavy ornate overmantel with a built-in picture. A heavy fire-side elbow chair stands above the fireplace. A quarter-circular, well-filled bookcase, built into the wall, reaches from* L *of the double doors to the upstage pillar of the alcove* L. *An oval table stands* L *of the hall alcove. There is a desk and desk chair up* LC. *The upstage wall of the alcove* L *has a long curved-top window without curtains. Under the window there is a small table. There is a table down* L *set out with drinks. An elbow chair stands below the downstage pillar of the alcove. A comfortable sofa stands at an angle* C, *with small tables* R, L *and above it. There is a telephone on the table above the sofa. The whole room is heavily carpeted and richly decorated with heavy, gilt, original paintings. There are electric wall brackets* R *and* L *of the fireplace, and table-lamps on the oval table up* C, *the desk and the table down* L. *There is a bell-lever at the fireplace.*

(*See the Ground Plan and Photograph of the Scene*)

When the CURTAIN *rises, it is about two-thirty.* CRESTWELL, *the butler, is standing at the desk. He is a good-looking man in the middle fifties. He carries a tray.* ALICE, *a young housemaid, is aged about eighteen. She is standing down* R, *emptying ashtrays into a dustpan.* CRESTWELL *collects two dirty cocktail glasses from the desk and puts them on his tray.*

---

*N.B. Paragraph 3 on page ii of this Acting Edition regarding photocopying and video-recording should be carefully read.

ALICE. . . . and just at the end of the film, he realizes that she is the one he's loved all along and they walk up a hill together hand in hand and the music gets louder and louder. . . .

CRESTWELL (*collecting the dirty glass from the table* L *of the sofa*) Thanks, Alice. I shan't have to see her now, shall I?

ALICE. She's lovely, Mr Crestwell. Really she is.

CRESTWELL. She'd better be.

ALICE. Don't you like her, Mr Crestwell?

CRESTWELL. How do I know? I've never clapped eyes on her.

ALICE. But you must have seen her in something.

CRESTWELL (*crossing to the table down* L *and collecting a dirty glass*) I've got better things to do with my spare time than to sit in the *Odeon* sucking sweets and gaping at a lot of nonsense.

ALICE. *Love is my Religion* is on in Deal all this week. It's one of her early ones, but it's gorgeous. I went on Thursday afternoon. (*She moves below the table* R *of the sofa*) She's this nun, you see . . .

CRESTWELL (*crossing and standing below the table* L *of the sofa*) Which nun?

ALICE. The one that gets captured by the Japanese.

CRESTWELL. Hurry up with those ashtrays or we shall all be captured by the Japanese. (*He moves* L *of the sofa to the table up* C)

ALICE. And they do the most terrible things to her but she won't tell where he is.

CRESTWELL (*collecting a dirty glass from the table up* C) Where who is?

ALICE. Don Lucas.

CRESTWELL. Get on with your work, Alice. They'll be in in a minute.

ALICE (*crossing to the table* L *of the sofa*) They're in love with one another in real life, her and Don Lucas. (*She empties the ashtray*) I read about it in *Screen Romances.*

CRESTWELL (*crossing to the mantelpiece and collecting a dirty glass*) Never mind about who she's in love with and who she isn't, it's no business of yours. And don't believe what you read in those movie magazines either—it's all a pack of lies cooked up to impress silly girls like you.

> (MRS MOXTON, *known as* MOXIE, *enters from the hall. She is a pleasant looking woman aged forty-six, and is simply dressed as befits a superior lady's-maid. Her expression, however, is grim.* ALICE *crosses to the table down* L *and empties the ashtray*)

(*To Moxie*) What's milady lost now?

MOXIE. The list for the church fête. She wants to show it to Lady Hayling. (*She looks on the table up* C *for Felicity's handbag, then moves above the right end of the sofa and looks on it*) I put it in her bag myself this morning. (*She sees the handbag on the left end of the sofa, crosses below the sofa, picks up the handbag and looks in it*)

ALICE (*moving down* LC) Can Maureen come up and help with the tea tomorrow afternoon, Mr Crestwell?

(MOXIE *gives Alice a look*)

CRESTWELL. Help with the tea? What on earth for?

ALICE. I could lend her a cap and apron. No-one would notice.

CRESTWELL. Two years ago, Alice, your sister Maureen was offered the job you've got now, wasn't she?

ALICE. Yes, Mr Crestwell.

CRESTWELL. And she turned up her nose at it because she said domestic service was common. Isn't that so?

ALICE (*meekly*) Yes, Mr Crestwell.

CRESTWELL. She is now assisting behind the bar at *The Fishermen's Rest* in Deal, which I presume she considers more aristocratic than Marshwood House. Isn't that so, Alice?

ALICE (*uncomfortably*) I'm sure I couldn't say, Mr Crestwell.

CRESTWELL (*moving down* R) Why then should this fastidious girl, this runner-up for the bathing beauty competition at Ramsgate, suddenly wish to don the garb of slavery?

ALICE. Well—I—you see . . .

CRESTWELL. Has she said to herself, "I know that they are short-handed at Marshwood on account of Amy having to visit her sick granny in Canterbury and May being in bed with shingles . . ."?

MOXIE (*putting the bag on the table* L *of the sofa*) Stop talking nonsense, you're keeping Alice from her work. (*She moves to the desk and looks in the desk drawers*)

CRESTWELL. Has she said to herself, "For the sake of Mr Crestwell who is rapidly going barmy, I will sacrifice my naughty pride and spring gladly into the breach"?

ALICE. I'm sure I don't know, Mr . . .

CRESTWELL (*thunderously*) The answer, Alice, is *no*. The answer Alice, is that your sister, like so many of her contemporaries, is a film-struck, good-for-nothing little fathead! And all that she wants to help with the tea for is to get a close-up view of Miss Miranda Frayle and probably ask for her autograph. And I tell you solemnly, here and now, that if she gets it, it will be over my—(*he crosses below the sofa to* R *of Alice*) dead body. (*He puts the tray of glasses on top of Alice's ashpan*)

MOXIE. Run along now, Alice—you've been standing about quite long enough.

ALICE (*over her shoulder*) Yes, Mrs Moxton.

(ALICE *crosses* C *below Moxie and exits to the hall*)

MOXIE. What's the sense of talking to the girl like that? She doesn't understand half you say.

CRESTWELL (*crossing to the table down* L) That is a cross I have learned to bear with fortitude, Dora. No-one understands half of what I say.

MOXIE. Then save your breath and say less.

CRESTWELL (*picking up an ashtray from the table down* L) What's the matter with you? (*He turns and moves down* LC) You've been snapping everybody's head off for the last three days.

MOXIE (*taking a list from one of the drawers*) Here it is.

CRESTWELL. What's up?

MOXIE (*crossing to the hall doors*) Nothing's up. I must take this through. Her ladyship's waiting for it.

CRESTWELL. Ever since the news came you've been behaving like a tragedy queen. It can't matter to you all that much.

MOXIE (*turning*) It does matter to me. (*She moves down* C) It matters to all of us.

CRESTWELL. You can't believe those movie magazines, you know.

MOXIE. I don't read movie magazines.

CRESTWELL. Oh yes, you do. I saw three of them in your room only last week.

MOXIE. What were you doing in my room?

CRESTWELL (*with dignity*) You asked me to fetch your work basket, and with my inherent chivalry, which all the disruptive forces of social revolution have been powerless to destroy, I nipped up three flights and got it for you.

MOXIE. I didn't ask you to go poking and prying about.

CRESTWELL (*patiently*) Your work basket, Dora, was on the table by your bed. Beside it were three magazines, *Screenland*, *Photoplay*, and *Love Stories of the Stars*. (*He crosses below Moxie to* R *of the sofa*) On the cover of the latter there was a full page photograph in colour of the future Countess of Marshwood in a two-piece bathing-suit, being warmly embraced by a gentleman in a one-piece bathing-suit.

MOXIE. Alice must have left them there when she was doing the room.

CRESTWELL. I accept your unconvincing explanation. (*He moves to the fireplace and puts the ashtray on the mantelpiece*)

MOXIE. I suppose it's only natural that I should want to see what the new mistress of the house looked like.

CRESTWELL (*moving down* R) This unwitting bit of espionage on my part took place last week, Dora, before any of us had the slightest idea that his lordship intended to marry again.

MOXIE (*crossing to* L *of Crestwell; angrily*) I'm surprised at you, I am really. You've been with the family longer than I have and you don't seem to mind this—this terrible thing a bit. All you do is to make jokes about it.

CRESTWELL. The trouble with you is you're too conservative.

MOXIE. Who did you vote for in the last election?

CRESTWELL. You don't have to be conservative to vote Conservative, you just plump for the lesser of two evils.

MOXIE. Why couldn't he pick someone of his own class? (*She turns to the sofa and arranges the cushions*)

CRESTWELL. Class! Oh dear, I've forgotten what the word means. Remind me to look it up in the crossword dictionary.

MOXIE (*over her shoulder*) You may have forgotten what it means, but I haven't.

CRESTWELL. That, Dora, is an admission of defeat. It proves that you have wilfully deafened yourself to the clarion call of progress.

MOXIE. Clarion call of fiddlesticks.

CRESTWELL. What's happened to your early dreams and ambitions—what's happened to your divine discontent?

MOXIE (*moving to* L *of Crestwell*) I never had any.

CRESTWELL. You'll be telling me in a minute that you are perfectly happy in the state in which it has pleased God to call you.

MOXIE. I wish you'd stop trying to be funny for one minute. I know you're making light of the whole business on purpose, pretending it doesn't matter, but I wish you—(*she takes her handkerchief from her pocket*) wouldn't—not to me anyhow—I really do wish you wouldn't. (*She moves to the sofa, sits and sobs*)

CRESTWELL (*gently*) Don't take it so hard. (*He moves to* R *of Moxie and pats her shoulder*) It may not be as bad as you think.

MOXIE (*looking up at him*) You hate it as much as I do, don't you?

CRESTWELL. Well, what if I do? There's no sense in bellyaching about it. The only thing is to look at it philosophically and hope for the best.

MOXIE. A common, painted hussy from Hollywood flaunting herself as the Countess of Marshwood, and you talk about hoping for the best.

CRESTWELL. Well, that's what her ladyship's trying to do. She's had Lady Hayling nagging at her all through lunch. She kept on trying to change the subject but it was no use.

MOXIE. Her ladyship's just as upset as we are, inside

CRESTWELL. Has she said so?

MOXIE. No. But I can tell.

CRESTWELL. Have you discussed it with her?

MOXIE (*snappily*) No, I have not.

CRESTWELL. All right—all right. Miss Miranda Frayle may not be all that common; she's English born anyhow—it says so in *Photoplay*.

MOXIE (*rising, crossing to* LC *and standing above the table* L *of the sofa*) I don't care if she was born in Timbuctoo. I don't care if her blood's blue, black or yellow. I don't care if she's English, French, Russian or Chinese. I only know that when she walks into this house I shall walk out.

CRESTWELL (*crossing below Moxie to the alcove table; dryly*) You'd better start packing. They'll be here at about six. (*He collects the ashtray from the alcove table*)

MOXIE (*turning to him; grimly*) I mean it.

CRESTWELL (*standing on the alcove step*) Of course, a great deal depends on what she's like.

MOXIE. He oughtn't to marry her whatever she's like.

CRESTWELL (*moving to* L *of Moxie*) This arbitrary point of view shocks me profoundly.

MOXIE. Does it indeed?

CRESTWELL (*tapping her shoulder*) What's happened to your *laissez faire?*

MOXIE. I expect I lost it along with my divine discontent.

(CRESTWELL *replaces the ashtray on the alcove table.* MOXIE *moves down* L.

FELICITY, COUNTESS OF MARSHWOOD, LADY HAYLING, ADMIRAL SIR JOHN HAYLING *and* THE HONOURABLE PETER INGLETON *enter from the hall.* FELICITY *is a well-preserved woman in the fifties. She has obviously been a beauty in her day, indeed a vestige of the maligned, foolish Twenties still clings to her.* LADY HAYLING, *also in the fifties, is a pleasant enough woman, but inclined to be didactic. The* ADMIRAL *is about sixty. He is typically a naval man with blue eyes and a direct manner.* PETER *might be anywhere between thirty-five and fifty. He is impeccably dressed and has a quizzical gleam in his eye.* LADY HAYLING *moves down* R. *The* ADMIRAL *moves* R *and stands above Lady Hayling.* PETER *stands above the right end of the sofa*)

FELICITY (*crossing above the sofa to* L *of it*) Couldn't you find it, Moxie, dear? (*She moves below the sofa*)

MOXIE (*crossing to Felicity and handing her the list*) Yes, Milady—here it is. (*She turns to go*)

(CRESTWELL *moves down* L)

FELICITY (*to Moxie and Crestwell*) Don't go, for heaven's sake, I shall need your help—yours, too, Crestwell. There's a full-blooded crisis on about the church fête. (*She sits on the sofa at the left end*) Everything's got to be changed round. Where's that horrid little map of the ground, Moxie?

MOXIE (*moving to the desk*) I think it's in the desk, Milady. (*She takes a small map from the desk drawer*)

(PETER *takes a cigarette from the box on the table above the sofa, and lights it*)

FELICITY (*picking up her spectacles from the table* L *of the sofa*) I may require you to go and murder Major Petherick, Crestwell.

CRESTWELL. Very good, Milady.

FELICITY. He has absolutely dug his feet in about the roundabouts. I've just been talking to him on the telephone. He was quite insufferable. (*She puts on her spectacles*)

MOXIE (*opening the map, moving to Felicity and handing it to her*) Here's the map, Milady. (*She moves below the chair down* L)

(PETER *moves above the left end of the sofa, leans over the back and looks at the map*)

PETER. What's that space there?

(LADY HAYLING *crosses and sits* R *of Felicity on the sofa. The* ADMIRAL *crosses and stands below the right end of the sofa*)

FELICITY. Mrs Burrage's clock golf and the tea tent. We can't possibly move that, it would drive everybody mad.

PETER (*pointing at the map*) What about there, then, right at the other end? Where all those little squiggles are.

FELICITY. Those little squiggles, Peter, are graves. We can't have a roundabout grinding out *Candy Kisses* all over the cemetery.

PETER (*pointing at the map*) There then.

FELICITY. Get your mind away from that corner, Peter. It's still church property. We know the fête is annual hell, but it isn't the Day of Judgement.

CRESTWELL. The only alternative, Milady, is to move the band.

ADMIRAL. That's out of the question. The brigadier wouldn't hear of it. You can't hustle the Royal Marines about from pillar to post at the last minute.

PETER. I always thought that was what Marines were for.

FELICITY (*handing the list to Moxie*) Read out the list, Moxie. (*She studies the map*) There might be something else that's movable.

MOXIE (*reading woodenly*) "Tombola—Mrs Edgecombe. Guessing the weight of the cake—Mrs Bryce. Miss Hodmarsh's Lucky Dip . . ."

PETER. I should never have suspected her of having one.

(MOXIE *looks at Peter*)

FELICITY. Do be quiet, Peter. Go on, Moxie.

MOXIE (*reading*) "Jumble Stall—Mrs Pollet and Mrs Dint. Cooling Drinks with the Stars—Miss Miranda Frayle . . ." (*She breaks off*)

FELICITY. That's not official yet because we haven't asked her, but I don't see how she can refuse, do you?

PETER. I should think it would be the least she could do.

LADY HAYLING. I wish it was.

FELICITY. Cynthia, we really can't go on about that any more —we've been at it all through lunch. Moxie, you must tell Mr Durham to paint the sign with her name, Miss Miranda Frayle, in absolutely enormous letters.

MOXIE (*in a stifled voice*) Yes, Milady. (*She turns and moves below the chair down* L)

FELICITY (*removing her spectacles and folding the map*) What's the matter, Moxie? (*She puts her spectacles on the table* L *of the sofa*)

MOXIE. Nothing, Milady. I've got a slight headache, that's all.

FELICITY. Have you had your lunch?

MOXIE. Yes, thank you, Milady.

FELICITY. Then give me that tiresome list and go and lie down for a little. There's some aspirin in my bathroom if you haven't got any.

MOXIE (*handing the list to Felicity*) Thank you, Milady. (*She crosses above the sofa to the hall doors*) Excuse me.

(MOXIE *exits hurriedly to the hall. The others look after her for a moment*)

FELICITY. Has anything particular happened to upset Moxie, Crestwell?

CRESTWELL. I think she has been feeling a bit under the weather for the last three days, Milady.

FELICITY. Oh, dear. I do hope she's not sickening for anything. You don't happen to remember how May's shingles started, do you?

CRESTWELL. I'm afraid not, Milady. One day she hadn't got them and the next day she had. It took us all by surprise.

FELICITY. I wonder if we ought to send for Doctor Partridge?

CRESTWELL. I think not, Milady. My impression is that Mrs Moxton's disorder is emotional rather than physical.

FELICITY. Emotional?

CRESTWELL. I believe that the unexpected news of his lordship's betrothal came as a great shock to her.

ADMIRAL. It came as a great shock to all of us.

FELICITY. Has she discussed it with you, Crestwell?

CRESTWELL. Hardly at all, Milady, until just now before you came in.

FELICITY. Without asking you to betray her confidence in any way, has she explained why she feels so very strongly about it?

CRESTWELL. As far as I could gather, Milady, I believe it is the social aspect of the situation that is upsetting her more than anything else.

FELICITY. You mean that she considers my son to be marrying beneath him?

CRESTWELL. That is so, Milady. I tried to reason with her, to coax her into a more tolerant frame of mind, to point out to her the changing values of this changing world, but, like Major Petherick and the roundabouts, she just dug her feet in.

FELICITY. Thank you, Crestwell.

(PETER *picks up the newspaper from the table above the sofa and studies the crossword puzzle*)

CRESTWELL (*moving to* L *of the sofa*) Will that be all. Milady?

FELICITY. Except for the roundabouts, yes. (*She hands the list and map to Crestwell*) You'd better take the list and the map to Mr Durham and see if he has any ideas.

CRESTWELL. Very good, Milady.

FELICITY. I have to see him after tea, anyhow. But he might be able to think up something in the meantime.

(CRESTWELL *crosses above the sofa and exits to the hall, closing the doors behind him.* LADY HAYLING *settles herself comfortably in the right corner of the sofa. The* ADMIRAL *moves to the fireplace, takes a cigarette from the box on the mantelpiece, and lights it.* PETER *moves to the desk and picks up a pencil*)

I don't know what I shall do without Crestwell. Do you remember how all through the war he and Moxie and I ran this house and dealt with all those brisk Waafs, and he never turned a hair. He was an A.R.P. Warden, too. I shall miss him horribly.

LADY HAYLING. Why should you do without him?

FELICITY. I can't take him away from Nigel. He belongs here.

(PETER *moves to the chair down* L, *sits and works at the crossword puzzle*)

LADY HAYLING. Are you so certain that Nigel will want you to go?

FELICITY. He won't say he wants me to go, but I don't approve of resident mothers-in-law. I had quite enough of that with Joan.

PETER. I shouldn't think that this one would be very like Joan.

FELICITY. Well, she couldn't be duller at any rate. Nobody could.

(*The* ADMIRAL *moves down* R *of the sofa*)

LADY HAYLING. Joan may have been dull, but she was at least a lady.

FELICITY (*laughing*) Really, Cynthia!

LADY HAYLING. You know perfectly well what I mean.

FELICITY. Yes, I know what you mean. Miss Miranda Frayle is a good actress and she has excellent legs, which means that she will probably move well, at any rate. Joan used to walk across a ballroom as though she were trudging through deep snow.

LADY HAYLING. But why should he want to marry this woman? He hasn't wanted to marry any of the others.

FELICITY. That's where you're wrong. He wanted to marry *all* the others. He has a tremendous sense of moral responsibility. Fortunately, most of them were married already.

ADMIRAL. Judy Lavenham wasn't.

FELICITY. Poor dear Judy was in quite a different category. By the time they met she was already practically nationalized.

LADY HAYLING (*shocked*) Felicity!

Felicity. Now, Joan had all the same instincts as Judy but neither the charm nor the courage to follow them. Happily dear Bogey Whittaker caught her on the hop before she had time to think, otherwise she'd be here now instead of in Kenya.

Lady Hayling. I cannot understand your attitude, Felicity. The fact that Nigel's first marriage was such a disaster should make you all the more anxious that his second should be a success.

Felicity. Nigel's first marriage was not a disaster, it was a triumph. To begin with it lasted only two years; it produced a son and heir, and disintegrated painlessly in the nick of time.

Admiral (*stubbing out his cigarette in the ashtray on the table down* R) The nick of time?

Felicity. Certainly. I was on the verge of strangling Joan with my bare hands when away she went. I am not a deeply religious woman, but I have always regarded Bogey Whittaker as a concrete proof of the efficacy of prayer.

Lady Hayling. I am perfectly aware that nowadays all social barriers are being swept away and that everybody is as good as everybody else, and that any suggestion of class distinction is laughed at . . .

Felicity. If you're aware of all that, what on earth are you making such a fuss about?

Lady Hayling. Because I don't believe it, any more than you do really in your heart. You know as well as I do that if Nigel is allowed to marry this synthetic, trumped-up creature it will be just one more nail in all our coffins.

Felicity (*laughing*) Dearest Cynthia. You really must not let righteous indignation play such hell with your syntax.

Lady Hayling. It's no good trying to discuss anything seriously with you, you're quite hopeless.

Felicity (*rising and moving to* L *of the sofa*) Do take Cynthia away, John. She's getting quite hoarse from barking up the wrong trees.

Lady Hayling. I'm merely saying what I think.

Felicity. Well, don't, dear. It's so exhausting. (*She moves above the sofa to* R *of the table up* C)

Lady Hayling. John agrees with me, at any rate—don't you, John?

Admiral. Of course, in my opinion we ought all to put our heads together while there's still time.

Peter. Like the Andrews Sisters.

Admiral. It's fairly obvious to me that Nigel must have been tricked into this in some way. (*He moves to the fireplace*) After all, he's no fool.

Felicity (*crossing to* L *of the Admiral*) John dear, he *is*. He's my own son and I ought to know.

Peter. I agree that Nigel has always been fairly idiotic about women, but it's reasonable to suppose that there must be something nice about her for him to have fallen in love with her in the first place.

LADY HAYLING. He was in love with Mrs Clifford Hargrave. I should like to know what was nice about her.

FELICITY (*moving above the right end of the sofa*) *Mr* Clifford Hargrave. (*She crosses above the sofa to* L *of it*)

LADY HAYLING (*turning away*) Really, Felicity!

FELICITY. But I mean it. He was a darling. Wasn't he, Peter?

PETER. A rather dim darling.

FELICITY. And he took it all so well, too.

ADMIRAL (*sarcastically*) Damned decent of him.

FELICITY. And he simply adored this house. (*To Peter*) We missed him dreadfully when it was all over.

(PETER *rises and moves down* L)

LADY HAYLING (*rising and moving down* C) Come along, John. (*She glances at her watch*) It's nearly half past three and you've got old Renshaw coming at four. (*She moves to* R *of Felicity and pats her arm*) See you at dinner. (*She crosses below Felicity to the french windows and waits for the Admiral*)

ADMIRAL (*crossing below the sofa to* R *of Felicity*) You know you can rely on us to back you up, Felicity, in whatever line you choose to take.

FELICITY (*affectionately*) Yes, dear John, of course I do. But I think in this instance that masterly inactivity is the best strategy. In fact we must study the chart and take our bearings before we set our course.

PETER. Anchors aweigh!

LADY HAYLING. Come along, John.

ADMIRAL. We'll be over for dinner at about eight-thirty. Keep in good heart, my dear.

(*The* ADMIRAL *pats Felicity gently on the shoulder, crosses to the french windows and exits with* LADY HAYLING)

FELICITY. Aye-aye! (*She crosses below the sofa to the fireplace*) I'm afraid I was beastly to poor Cynthia. But she really maddens me at moments. (*She takes a cigarette from the box on the mantelpiece, and lights it*)

PETER. Personally I think they're both cracking bores and I always have.

FELICITY (*moving down* R) Perhaps they are, but you see they're such old friends. I've known them for so many years. Cynthia, of course, since we were at school together.

PETER. I'll bet she was top of the class in algebra and captain of the lacrosse team.

FELICITY. She also played Bolingbroke in *Richard the Second* and her wig fell off.

PETER. She seems to have put it back.

(MOXIE *enters quietly from the hall and stands in the open doorway*)

FELICITY (*turning and moving to the fireplace*) What is it, Moxie? I haven't forgotten anything important, have I?

MOXIE. No, Milady. I just wanted to speak to you, that's all— I'll come back later.

PETER (*moving to the desk*) It's all right, Moxie dear. (*He puts the paper and pencil on the desk*) I'm going to the village and you can have a clear field.

MOXIE (*in rather a choked voice*) It doesn't matter, sir—I'd rather come back later.

(MOXIE *exits hurriedly to the hall, closing the door behind her*)

FELICITY (*moving down* RC) Oh dear.

PETER (*moving down* C) She's obviously in a state.

FELICITY. I wish she wouldn't be, I really do. It's so catching. Why do you suppose she's taking it so dreadfully to heart?

PETER (*crossing below Felicity to* R) Have you talked to her about it much?

FELICITY. No. Whenever I mention it she changes the subject. She's very deeply angry I think.

PETER. With Nigel?

FELICITY. Yes. She adores him. She always has, ever since she first came here. You know, he was only fifteen then and they used to go to matinées together and have tea afterwards at *Gunters.*' I think she feels that he's letting down the side.

PETER (*sitting in the chair* R) Maybe she's right.

FELICITY. There is still just a hope that she's wrong.

PETER. I think it's a pretty slim one.

FELICITY. I don't see why. After all, it isn't the first time an English peer has married an actress. In the old days they never stopped. (*She sits on the sofa*) Of course I expect there were always family rows and upsets, but it nearly always turned out all right in the long run. Look at dear Gloria Bainbridge, buried alive in Lincolnshire and absolutely indefatigable, and Lily Grantworth with all those muscular little boys. I think the aristocracy, what's left of it, owes a great deal to the theatrical profession.

PETER. Hollywood isn't quite the same as the theatrical profession. It's more flamboyant.

FELICITY. I can't see that that matters. We live in an age of publicity and we might just as well enjoy it.

PETER. You know perfectly well that you hate it. You loathe being blinded by flash bulbs whenever you go to a first night and being caught by a candid camera at the *Dorchester* with your mouth full of asparagus.

FELICITY. That was for charity. Anyhow, what about you?

You're constantly being photographed seeing people off at railway stations and airports, and you revel in it.

PETER. It's part of my job, and I don't revel in it, I detest it. You can't run a travel bureau without advertising.

FELICITY. One of the worst aspects of modern English life, is that so many of one's friends have to work, and they're so bad at it.

PETER. The Ingleton Rail-Sea-and-Air office is a byword of brisk efficiency.

FELICITY. Only because of that dusty looking girl with glasses. If she weren't there you'd never get anyone further than Folkestone.

PETER. I fail to see why you should attack me just because your son's marrying a film star and your maid's upset about it.

FELICITY (*rising and moving to* L *of the sofa*) Oh, Peter, I'm upset too. I told you before, it's catching. (*She moves above the sofa*) The last three days have been hell. I've had Cynthia Hayling rasping my nerves like a buzz saw, Moxie plunged in gloom, Crestwell looking sardonic and an insufferable letter from Rose Eastry telling me to stand firm. (*She crosses to the fireplace and stands gazing into it*)

PETER. What's it to do with her?

FELICITY (*turning*) Go and ask her. She's your aunt, too.

PETER. Only in a roundabout way.

FELICITY. If I hear that word again I shall shriek.

PETER. Calm down, dear, and concentrate on the problem in hand.

FELICITY. That's exactly what I'm trying to do, but everybody keeps going on and on about it so. (*She moves to* L *of Peter*) I've made up my mind to accept Miss Miranda Frayle without prejudice, however ghastly she turns out to be.

PETER. She may not be ghastly at all. She may be absolutely enchanting. She may be simple and unaffected and fill the house all day long with her spontaneous laughter.

FELICITY. That's what I dread most.

PETER. Or she may be a little sad, a little weary and bruised by life, like she was in *Be Still Foolish Heart*.

FELICITY. Was that the one where she got so dreadfully knocked about by Edward G. Robinson?

PETER. No. That was *Women Laugh at Love*.

FELICITY (*moving and sitting on the sofa*) It's the suddenness of the whole thing that's really upsetting me more than anything else.

PETER. Is it?

FELICITY. Yes, Peter, it is, and you needn't look quizzical, either. That's my story and I'm sticking to it.

PETER. Very wise.

FELICITY. I have purposely refrained from analysing my emotions and rooting about among my innermost feelings, because if

I did I should probably discover that I am a good deal more unhappy than I think I am.

PETER. Wiser still.

FELICITY (*rising and moving down* LC; *vehemently*) *Of course* I would rather it hadn't happened. *Of course* I would rather he had chosen someone less glittery and spectacular, someone less flagrantly unsuitable to run Marshwood and be a good step-mother to Jeremy.

PETER. Of course.

FELICITY (*moving to the desk*) And of course it would have been more convenient and pleasant if he had picked someone who likes the things he likes and knows about the things he knows about.

PETER (*rising*) Someone of his own class, in fact?

FELICITY (*stubbing out her cigarette in the ashtray on the desk*) Yes—if you must have it—someone of his own class. There. Now are you satisfied?

PETER (*moving and sitting on the sofa at the right end*) Not satisfied exactly, but definitely reassured.

FELICITY (*moving above the left end of the sofa; crossly*) I see nothing to be reassured about. You have merely forced me to say something that I have been valiantly trying not to admit, even to myself. It's very unkind of you.

PETER. Never mind. Press on, Felicity. You're doing splendidly.

FELICITY. Don't laugh at me. It's all quite beastly, and you know it. (*She moves to* L *of the sofa*) My instincts are at war with my reason.

PETER. Like Moxie.

FELICITY. Certainly. Moxie, too, belongs to something that's over and done with. That's what's making her miserable.

PETER. What about Crestwell?

FELICITY. How do you mean, what about Crestwell?

PETER. The same thing applies to him.

FELICITY. Crestwell is not emotional and Moxie is, he's also very adaptable and knows more about what's going on in the world than all of us put together. You should hear what he has to say about Social Revolution and the United Nations and the Decline of the West. It's fascinating.

PETER. How does he feel about Danny Kaye?

FELICITY. He reads everything, too, from *The New Statesman* to the *Daily Worker*. (*She moves to the upstage pillar of the alcove and leans against it in the sunshine*)

PETER. A fairly small range.

FELICITY. Moxie, of course, sticks to *The Times* and remains bewildered.

(*The telephone rings*)

Answer it, Peter, there's a dear. (*She moves to the french windows*) It's probably the Press again. They've been ringing up all day.

You can evade them with more authority than I can. (*She gazes out into the garden*)

(PETER *edges along the sofa, leans over the back and lifts the receiver*)

PETER. There I think you underrate yourself. (*Into the telephone*) Hello. . . . Yes, this is two-one-five-eight. . . . Yes—hold the line for a moment. (*To Felicity*) It's for you—a personal call from London.

(FELICITY *turns and moves to the rostrum step*)

FELICITY (*whispering*) Ask who it is.

PETER (*into the telephone*) Who wishes to speak to her? . . . Oh—all right—hold on. (*To Felicity*) It's the prodigal son himself.

FELICITY (*moving below the sofa*) Nigel! Oh dear. (*She takes the receiver from Peter and sits* L *of him on the sofa. Into the telephone*) Hello. . . . Yes, speaking. . . . (*To Peter*) The line's terrible, it sounds as though someone were snoring. (*Into the telephone*) Hello—hello—Nigel? . . . Yes, dear, of course it is. . . . What? . . . Speak louder. I can't hear a word. . . . (*To Peter*) He can't hear me either. (*Into the telephone*) Where are you? . . . I said *where are you?* . . . Oh, I see—you're just leaving now. . . . Lovely, darling. How are you—both? . . . No, dear, I said *how are you both?* . . . I'm doing my best, I'm screaming like a Banshee. . . . *Banshee*, darling. . . . B for bottle, A for Andalusia, N for Nebuchadnezzar. . . . No. . . .

(PETER *laughs*)

Nebuchadnezzar—N for nobody. . . . It doesn't matter. . . . It's not in the least important—I was only trying to explain what I was screaming like. . . . (*To Peter*) I'm going mad.

PETER. Jiggle the thing.

FELICITY. If I jiggle the thing I shall be cut off. Ah, that's better—the snoring's stopped. (*Into the telephone*) That's better—I can hear you now—can you hear me? . . . Good. . . . Oh, what a shame. . . . I expect it was because she was in a strange bed. (*She covers the mouthpiece with her hand. To Peter*) I know I shouldn't have said that, he'll think I was being critical. (*Into the telephone*) Very well, darling. . . . No—nobody but Peter and the Haylings—I thought you'd like to be quiet on your first evening. . . . Does she play Canasta? . . . Oh—never mind—we can all teach her—it will be lovely. . . . You don't have to have a card sense for Canasta, it's at least eighty per cent luck. . . . All right, darling, it really doesn't matter, it was just an idea. . . . Very well, we'll expect you between six and seven. . . . Of course I am, I'm sure she's charming. . . . (*To Peter*) I shouldn't have said that either, it sounded patronizing. (*Into the telephone*) No, it wasn't in the least important. . . . It sounded like Nebuchadnezzar because it was Nebuchadnezzar. . . . I really can't explain now, it's too complicated. . . . All right, darling. (*She hands the receiver to Peter*)

(Peter *leans over the back of the sofa and replaces the receiver*)

That was one of the most idiotic conversations I've ever had in my life.

Peter. Did he sound cheerful?

Felicity. A little irritable, I thought, but that might have been the telephone.

Peter. I expect he was nervous.

Felicity. I wasn't beastly to him, was I? I mean I didn't sound cross or anything?

Peter (*rising suddenly and affectionately kissing her*) No, dear, you were very, very good. I know it's horrid for you and I do sympathize, really I do. (*He crosses below Felicity to* L *of the sofa*)

Felicity. Well, please don't, Peter. Even a kindly look would undermine me at the moment. It's a pity the silly woman can't play Canasta, I was relying on it. This evening's going to be hell. Be a dear and go and find Moxie—I'd better get that over—she's probably hovering.

Peter. All right. (*He crosses above the sofa to the hall doors then stops, turns and stands above the left end of the sofa*) If you fail to cheer her up, tell her I'll drive her into Dover before tea. She dearly loves a little outing.

Felicity. I really don't think that will be necessary, a nice heart-to-heart will probably do the trick.

(Moxie *enters from the hall and stands in the doorway. She is quite calm but her expression is set*)

Oh, Moxie.

Moxie. I'm sorry, Milady.

Peter. It's all right, Moxie, I'm just going.

(Peter *crosses and exits by the french windows. There is a pause*)

Felicity (*kindly*) You look dreadfully grim, Moxie. What is it that's worrying you?

Moxie (*moving down* R; *grimly*) The thought of what I have to say to you, Milady. That's what's worrying me.

Felicity. Surely whatever you have to say to me can't be as awful as all that?

Moxie. I'm afraid it is.

Felicity (*patting the sofa by her side*) Sit down, dear, and relax a bit before you say anything at all.

Moxie. I'd rather stand, really I would. If I sat down I might cry and make a fool of myself. (*She pauses. With a great effort*) I'm afraid I have to leave you, Milady.

Felicity. Leave me? Why, Moxie—what on earth . . . ?

Moxie. At once, Milady—today. I've had some bad news.

FELICITY. Oh, my dear, I'm so awfully sorry—what is it?

MOXIE. It's my aunt, Milady—my mother's sister—she's very seriously ill and she's all alone. . . .

FELICITY. Where?

MOXIE (*after a slight hesitation*) Southsea.

FELICITY. Why is she all alone? Surely she must have someone to look after her?

MOXIE. Her husband looked after her, Milady—but—but—he died suddenly two days ago. I've just had a telegram from one of the neighbours.

FELICITY. And you have to leave at once?

MOXIE. Yes, Milady.

FELICITY. Oh, poor Moxie, how horrid for you. When do you think you'll be able to come back?

MOXIE. That's just it, Milady. I shan't be able to come back.

FELICITY. What!

MOXIE. You see, she's all alone—and she may just sort of linger on for years.

FELICITY. Do you mean to say that you want to leave me for good—now—this minute?

MOXIE. It isn't that I want to, Milady—do please believe that—it's that I must.

FELICITY. But this aunt of yours, what's the matter with her? What's she suffering from?

MOXIE. I don't rightly know, Milady. The doctors don't seem to have been able to make up their minds.

FELICITY. Couldn't she go to a hospital?

MOXIE. Oh no—she can't be moved.

FELICITY. And her husband who looked after her—what did he die of so very suddenly?

MOXIE. He was run over, Milady. (*She pauses*) By an army lorry.

FELICITY (*inexorably*) Where?

MOXIE. Just opposite the South Parade pier.

FELICITY. How do you know all this?

MOXIE. It was in the telegram.

FELICITY. Your aunt must have very extravagant neighbours.

MOXIE (*dimly*) Yes, Milady.

FELICITY. Moxie, how long have you been with me?

MOXIE. Twenty years. I came to Marshwood as housemaid in October nineteen thirty-one.

FELICITY. And you became my personal maid in nineteen thirty-three.

MOXIE. Yes.

FELICITY. And you've been my personal maid and my personal friend and part of the family ever since.

MOXIE (*looking away; distressed*) Yes, Milady.

Felicity. So we have lived together, travelled together, laughed together and gossiped together for approximately nineteen years.

Moxie. Yes, Milady.

Felicity. Can it be that during all that long time, Moxie, you have looked upon me as a drivelling idiot?

Moxie (*breaking down*) I'm sorry, Milady. (*She droops her head and looks at the floor*) I knew it was no use—I knew you wouldn't believe it.

Felicity. I think it was the army lorry that did it really. You're a terribly bad liar—I've noticed it on the telephone. (*She pauses*) You're upset about his lordship's marriage. That's the trouble, isn't it?

Moxie. Yes—yes, that's the trouble.

Felicity. You seriously wish to leave me because of it?

Moxie. Yes please, Milady.

Felicity. But why, Moxie dear? Why should it matter to you so desperately?

Moxie. Please let me go, Milady, and don't ask me to explain. I can't stay here—really I can't.

Felicity. But you won't have to stay here. Not for long, at any rate. I intend to go away myself at the earliest opportunity, and you naturally will leave with me.

Moxie. It's impossible, Milady. I must leave at once.

Felicity. But why?

Moxie (*gazing out front*) I have my reasons.

Felicity. And you won't tell me what they are?

Moxie. I can't, Milady. I really can't.

Felicity (*rising and moving down* LC) In that case there isn't anything more to be said, is there?

Moxie (*near to tears*) Oh, Milady.

Felicity (*moving to the desk and turning*) Obviously I can't force you to stay if you don't want to, nor can I compel you to explain if you have decided not to. (*She moves down* LC) I'm feeling angry at the moment, naturally enough, but unfortunately I know that the anger is only temporary. (*She moves to* R *of the desk*) It will pass inevitably in a little while and leave me bewildered, and sad, and bitterly, bitterly disappointed. (*She picks up the newspaper*) Come and say good-bye to me when you've packed. (*She throws the newspaper on to the desk*)

Moxie. Very well, Milady. (*She moves miserably towards the hall door*)

Felicity (*crossing quickly to Moxie and taking her by the hands*) Oh, Moxie, Moxie—this is too utterly fantastic—I can't possibly just let it happen without doing everything in my power to prevent it. (*She leads* Moxie *down* L) Please, please tell me why you feel that you have to leave me, so obviously against your will—I promise you I'll try to understand whatever it is—please, Moxie.

MOXIE (*withdrawing from Felicity and moving a little* L) I can't—it's too humiliating—I'm so ashamed.

FELICITY (*a thought striking her*) It isn't Nigel, is it? I mean, it isn't that he has ever . . . ?

MOXIE (*horrified*) Oh, no—no—of course it isn't.

FELICITY. Is it—is it perhaps that you love him—more than you can help?

MOXIE (*pulling herself together*) No, Milady—(*she moves to* L *of Felicity*) it's nothing like that—I swear it isn't. Of course I love his lordship. I've loved him ever since he was a boy—but not like that.

FELICITY. We're all worried about this sudden engagement. But we really must all make an effort to face the situation calmly and sensibly. After all, the world has changed a great deal in our lifetime, Moxie; lots of things that mattered dreadfully when we were young, don't matter at all any more. For all we know Miranda Frayle may be simple and kind and absolutely charming, and the only really important thing is that she should make him happy, isn't it?

MOXIE. She won't.

FELICITY. We can't prove that though, can we?

MOXIE (*crossing below Felicity to* R *and standing with her back to her*) If you searched the whole wide world with a tooth comb you couldn't find anybody less fitted to be his lordship's wife and the mistress of this house.

FELICITY. Why are you so sure? How do you know?

MOXIE (*turning*) Because, Milady, Miss Miranda Frayle happens to be my young sister.

CURTAIN

SCENE 2

SCENE—*The same. Two hours later.*

When the CURTAIN *rises a small circular table with a tray of tea for two stands below the right arm of the sofa.* FELICITY *is seated on the sofa at the right end.* PETER *is wandering about with a cup and saucer in his hand. There is a silence as he moves to the table up* C, *turns and crosses down* L.

FELICITY. I do wish you'd sit down, Peter. Nothing can be achieved by you charging about the room like a sort of Dodgem.

PETER (*crossing to* L *of the sofa*) What on earth's a Dodgem?

FELICITY. One of those little motor cars you go on in Margate and bang into everybody.

Peter. I haven't banged into anybody yet.

Felicity. We must concentrate. This is a serious crisis.

Peter. If we concentrate until we're blue in the face we shan't get any further. There's only one possible solution and you know it. You must go abroad immediately and take Moxie with you.

Felicity. That's not a solution at all, merely a temporary measure. And it's quite out of the question for me to go abroad immediately. My passport's in London and there are currency regulations. I used up my allocation in February and even then I had to borrow from Henrietta.

Peter. You must borrow from her again.

Felicity. She's in Morocco.

Peter (*crossing above the sofa and standing up* R) What's wrong with Morocco?

Felicity. Even if I went to the Barrier Reef, I couldn't stay there indefinitely. Besides, Moxie can't stand hot climates. She breaks out in a rash.

Peter (*crossing above the sofa to* LC) Well, send *her* away then, send her somewhere nice and cool.

Felicity. I've told you once and for all that I am not going to be parted from Moxie. I couldn't live without her and I don't intend to try.

Peter (*crossing to the tea-table, placing his cup on it and picking up a sandwich*) It may not be for long. We may be able to dissuade Nigel from marrying this tiresome woman and then she could go back to Hollywood and nobody need ever know.

Felicity. And how do you propose to go about dissuading him?

Peter (*crossing down* LC) Surely when he knows that his prospective sister-in-law is his mother's maid, it will shake him a bit?

Felicity. I don't see why.

Peter (*thoughtfully*) What was their name, their family name, I mean?

Felicity. Birch. They had a grocer's shop in Nightingale Lane between Brixton and Clapham; Freda, that's my future daughter-in-law, was the flighty one; Moxie married Moxton, Edith Harringworth's chauffeur. They had a child but it died, then Moxton died, too, so she went back to the shop and her mother.

Peter. And Freda?

Felicity. Oh, Freda had upped and left home long before then. Apparently she started making a beast of herself quite early.

Peter. In what way?

Felicity. Oh, the usual way. She kept on almost having babies but not quite.

Peter. Lack of concentration. (*He crosses to the sofa and sits on it,* L *of Felicity*)

Felicity. Then there was apparently a terrible scene and the mother had a stroke and Freda beetled off to America with a theatrical agent called Greenberg. That was the last Moxie saw of her.

PETER. Did the mother die?

FELICITY. Yes, in nineteen thirty-one, and the shop failed and Moxie came here as housemaid in the following October.

PETER (*thoughtfully*) Twenty years is a long time.

FELICITY. Time enough to forge bonds of loyalty and affection that are impossible to break.

PETER. Perhaps Freda—Miranda—whatever her name is—wouldn't recognize her.

FELICITY. Of course she would. Moxie's hardly changed at all.

PETER (*rising and moving down* LC) She could change though, couldn't she?

FELICITY. How do you mean?

PETER. I have an idea.

FELICITY (*sarcastically*) Disguise her I suppose.

PETER (*moving down* L) No. Promote her, that's the first thing, the disguise part can come later.

FELICITY. Oh, Peter.

PETER. No—wait a minute—it could be done, I'm sure it could.

FELICITY. What do you propose to do? Pop a tiara on her head and pretend she's the Duchess of Devonshire?

PETER (*crossing above the sofa up* R) Of course not, don't be so silly—but it would be possible.

FELICITY (*exasperated*) What would be possible?

PETER (*moving to* L *of the sofa*) As I see it, the crux of this whole situation is that Moxie is a domestic servant, a lady's maid, in fact, a social inferior.

FELICITY. There's nothing inferior about Moxie, social or otherwise.

PETER. All right, all right—I couldn't agree with you more—but that's beside the point.

FELICITY. What did you mean about promoting her?

PETER. Step her up—make her your companion, or your secretary.

FELICITY. But she presses my clothes and does my hair and brings me things on trays.

PETER. She doesn't do those things in public, I presume?

FELICITY. And what about Nigel? What would he say?

PETER. I should think if anything Nigel would be delighted (*He moves down* L) After all, she's going to be his sister.

FELICITY. Oh dear!

PETER (*crossing to* L *of her*) Did I detect in that exclamation a faint echo of old world snobbery, Felicity?

FELICITY. Of course, you didn't. It's only that it's all so idiotic, so inconsistent. Moxie is Moxie. Why should it make any difference whether she's called my maid or my secretary?

PETER. Why indeed? But it does. One must face facts. (*He sits* L *of Felicity on the sofa*) Nobody would think twice for instance if you took young Stephen Bristow to the opening night of the Ballet and to the *Savoy Grill* afterwards, would they?

FELICITY. Of course they wouldn't. He's a very charming boy.

PETER. But you wouldn't take Crestwell, would you?

FELICITY. Crestwell can't bear the Ballet. He says it's decadent.

PETER. The fact remains you wouldn't take him. It would embarrass him and you. It would also, very slightly, embarrass your friends. Stephen Bristow is the son of a tobacconist in Folkestone. Crestwell is the son of a police constable in Sevenoaks. (*He rises and crosses to* LC) As far as actual class goes there is nothing to choose between them. They are both hard-working, decent Englishmen, but one happens to be a golf instructor, and the other a butler, and the social abyss yawning between them, even in these democratic days, is still unbridgeable.

FELICITY. I still don't see how the present problem can be solved by making Moxie my secretary. She can't do shorthand or type, she can't even spell very well.

PETER. Neither can you.

FELICITY. But everybody knows her as my maid. They'd all think I was dotty if I suddenly said she was my secretary.

PETER. Companion then.

FELICITY. Where do companions eat?

PETER. Presumably with the people they're being companions to. Where is she now?

FELICITY. Upstairs in her room. I made her promise not to budge until I had had time to consider the situation from every angle.

PETER. Secretary-companion. She must be entirely re-dressed.

FELICITY. Oh, Peter, she'll never agree to it in a thousand years.

PETER (*crossing above the sofa to* R *of it*) I don't see why.

FELICITY. She's a woman of considerable pride. She will bitterly resent the idea of stepping out of her own *milieu* in order to be socially acceptable to her own sister.

PETER. Let's ask her anyhow.

FELICITY. Well, I think before we say anything to her I should like Crestwell's opinion. Ring the bell.

(PETER *moves to the fireplace and rings the bell*)

PETER. We could always make a family party of it and pretend that he's your long lost cousin from South Africa.

FELICITY. Don't be so idiotic.

PETER (*crossing below the sofa to* LC) I bet you anything you like I can make her absolutely unrecognizable. It's only a question of make-up really and doing her hair.

FELICITY. Don't be too carried away now, Peter. We're not planning charades. I won't have Moxie made a fool of.

PETER. There's no question of making a fool of her. It seems to me to be a very sensible way out of a tricky situation. Why should she object to being moved a step up in the social scale?

FELICITY. Because it's being done for the wrong reasons.

(CRESTWELL *enters from the hall. He opens the doors and leaves them open*)

CRESTWELL. You rang, Milady?

FELICITY. Yes, Crestwell. Is Mrs Moxton in her room?

CRESTWELL (*moving below the right end of the sofa*) Yes, Milady. She looked depressed so I sent her up a cup of tea.

FELICITY. How thoughtful of you, Crestwell.

CRESTWELL. I popped in to see her myself a short while ago and she perked up no end. She was just starting *The Times* crossword. I helped her a bit with it. She's quick as a knife on the clues but her spelling handicaps her terribly.

FELICITY. Oh.

PETER. You didn't happen to get "one down", did you? It's been driving me mad. It's six letters and I know it's a quotation from Milton.

CRESTWELL. The word is "nursed", sir. It's *Lycidas*. "For we were nursed upon the self-same hill."

PETER. Very appropriate. Thank you, Crestwell. (*He moves to the desk and makes an entry on the crossword puzzle*)

FELICITY. I have been thinking for some time of making a change in the household, Crestwell.

CRESTWELL. A change, Milady?

FELICITY. And I wanted to ask your opinion before I decide definitely. It concerns Moxie.

CRESTWELL. Yes, Milady?

(PETER *moves to the downstage pillar of the alcove, and leans against it*)

FELICITY. I wish to—to promote her—to alter her status. I was wondering how such a change would affect the other servants.

CRESTWELL. Well, there's only the cook to be considered seriously, Milady. May is occupied with her shingles at the moment; Amy and Alice don't count and I don't think that young Frank will be with us long anyhow.

FELICITY. Why not?

CRESTWELL. He is not happy in his work, Milady. Like so many of the young people of today, he holds very definite views on social equality. He feels that all menial tasks should be done by somebody else.

PETER. And the cook?

CRESTWELL. A reasonable woman up to a point, sir. Sometimes temperamental when time or circumstances thwart her endeavours, but by no means deaf to entreaty.

Felicity. Is she fond of Moxie?

Crestwell. Fond would be an overstatement, Milady. She respects her and occasionally tells her fortune with tea leaves, but I wouldn't describe their relationship as exactly intimate.

Felicity. What would she do if Moxie ceased to be part of the domestic staff and became my secretary?

Crestwell (*incredulously*) Secretary, Milady?

Felicity. Well—companion-secretary.

Crestwell. To what degree would such a metamorphosis affect the *status quo*, Milady?

Felicity. Well, I don't know really—I mean that would all have to be gone into very carefully.

Crestwell. Meals, for instance?

Felicity (*helplessly*) Oh dear—that is a problem, isn't it?

Crestwell. A problem certainly, but not an insoluble one. I presume that she could eat in the dining-room when you were *en famille* as it were?

Felicity (*looking at Peter*) Yes—I suppose so—yes, of course she could.

Crestwell. And on other, more formal occasions, she could have a tray upstairs. Might I suggest that we turn what used to be the Japanese room into a private sitting-room for her? Nobody ever uses it now and besides having a very agreeable view it would consolidate her position.

(Felicity *looks at* Peter, *who smiles*)

Felicity. What a wonderful idea, Crestwell. You don't think she'd be too lonely?

Crestwell. That is something we all have to face at one time or another, Milady. Superior rank invariably carries with it its own burdens. I am told that newly created naval commanders are frequently desolate when promotion snatches them from the dusty arena of the communal wardroom.

Felicity. I hadn't visualized Moxie as a naval commander exactly.

Crestwell. Nevertheless the analogy is not too far-fetched, Milady.

Felicity. You haven't yet answered my original question. What do you think of the idea, Crestwell?

Crestwell. May I ask if you have discussed it with Mrs Moxton herself?

Peter. Not yet. We wanted to get your reactions first.

Felicity. You think she won't agree?

Crestwell. I think, taking into consideration the very special circumstances, she might.

Peter. How much do you know, Crestwell?

CRESTWELL. In common with most of the human race, sir, I know very little but imagine I know a great deal.

FELICITY. Dear Crestwell, don't be evasive please, this is a crisis.

CRESTWELL. I suspected as much, Milady.

FELICITY (*firmly*) Miss Miranda Frayle, his lordship's intended bride, happens to be Mrs Moxton's sister.

CRESTWELL. Thank you, Milady. You may rely on my discretion.

FELICITY. You already guessed it?

CRESTWELL. By simple deduction and putting two and two together I had arrived at the conclusion that there was something a bit dodgy going on.

FELICITY. You were quite right, Crestwell. Nothing indeed could be dodgier.

(PETER *laughs at Felicity*)

CRESTWELL. A coincidence in the best tradition of English High Comedy, Milady. Consider how delightfully Mr Somerset Maugham would handle the situation.

PETER. I can think of other writers who wouldn't exactly sneeze at the idea.

CRESTWELL. If I may say so, sir, our later playwrights would miss the more subtle nuances. They are all too brittle. Comedies of manners swiftly become obsolete when there are no longer any manners.

FELICITY. Will you help us, Crestwell?

CRESTWELL. In what way, Milady?

FELICITY. In any way you can. You are a wise man and an exceedingly persuasive one.

CRESTWELL. Thank you, Milady.

FELICITY. I shall never forget how you managed that dreadful Waaf who took to the bottle and kept on disappearing on her bicycle in the middle of the night.

CRESTWELL (*picking up the tea-table and tray*) That was more moral blackmail than persuasion, Milady. (*He moves to the hall doors*)

FELICITY. Crestwell, will you go and ask Moxie to come down?

CRESTWELL (*over his shoulder*) Very good, Milady.

(PETER *laughs.*
CRESTWELL *exits to the hall*)

FELICITY. Try not to enjoy the situation too whole-heartedly, Peter.

(CRESTWELL *puts down the table and tray and closes the hall doors.* FELICITY *leans over the back of the sofa and takes a cigarette from the box on the table above the sofa*)

PETER (*crossing to Felicity*) I can't imagine why you don't marry Crestwell, Felicity. (*He lights her cigarette with his lighter*) It would simplify everything.

Felicity. It's terribly upsetting really.

Peter. It needn't be, if it's properly handled. (*He perches himself on the left arm of the sofa*)

Felicity. It's Moxie that I am worrying about. I've suddenly realized something, something curiously humiliating.

Peter. What?

Felicity. I don't really know her at all.

Peter. What on earth do you mean?

Felicity. She knows me all right, there's no doubt about that. She has studied my moods and obeyed my wishes. She knows all my problems and all my relations, in fact there are certain aspects of me that she alone knows. She has nursed me through illnesses, she has seen me in tears, she has seen me dressed and undressed, with my face plastered with grease or made up to the eyes. And only once, in nineteen years, have I ever seen her in her dressing-gown and that was in the station hotel in Genoa when I had ptomaine poisoning from eating bad fish.

Peter (*moving down* L *taking a cigarette from his case, and lighting it*) Surely true knowledge of character doesn't necessarily depend on constantly seeing people in their dressing-gowns?

Felicity (*rising and moving up* R *of the sofa*) She has done her job faithfully and well, she has given me devoted service, she has comforted me and cossetted me and received all my confidences for all those long years, and until today I didn't even know that she had a sister. (*She crosses above the sofa to* L *of it*)

Peter. If she was ashamed of her, if she had cut her out of her life, it was quite natural that she shouldn't discuss her, or even mention her.

Felicity. I've told Moxie many things that I was ashamed of.

(Moxie, *followed by* Crestwell, *enters from the hall.* Crestwell *closes the door.* Felicity *moves to the desk and stubs out her cigarette in the ashtray on it*)

Moxie. Crestwell says that you wish to speak to me, Milady.

Felicity (*moving down* C) Yes, Moxie, I do, most urgently. Will you sit down? (*She indicates the sofa*) On the sofa.

Moxie (*moving below the sofa*) Very well, Milady. (*She sits on the sofa at the left end*)

Felicity. Crestwell, please sit down, too. This is a family conference and it can't possibly be dealt with satisfactorily if everybody is standing about.

Crestwell (*moving below the sofa*) Very good, Milady.

Felicity (*indicating the chair down* L) Peter?

Peter (*rising*) All right. (*He sits in the chair down* L) I feel as though we ought to have pencils and paper.

(FELICITY *crosses and sits in the chair* R. CRESTWELL *sits* R *of Moxie on the sofa*)

FELICITY. Now then, Moxie dear. I have explained the situation confidentially to Mr Peter. I had to discuss it with somebody and he is an old friend whose discretion can be completely relied on.

MOXIE. I quite understand, Milady.

FELICITY. Crestwell also. But as a matter of fact he had already guessed.

MOXIE (*looking balefully at Crestwell*) Had he indeed, Milady?

CRESTWELL. A process of natural deduction, Dora, cause and effect, you know.

MOXIE. I don't know any such thing. But I do know about people nosing about and not minding their own business.

FELICITY. Moxie, you mustn't be cross with Crestwell. He is eager to help us in any way he can.

MOXIE. Very kind of him, I'm sure.

FELICITY. The thought of you leaving Marshwood and me for any reason except that you were unhappy here fills me with dismay.

MOXIE. But that is the reason, Milady. I shall be unhappy here. I couldn't very well be anything else in the circumstances.

FELICITY. I fully appreciate that, Moxie, which is why I have decided, after careful deliberation, to alter the circumstances.

MOXIE. May I ask how, Milady?

FELICITY. I wish you from now onwards to cease being my personal maid and become my companion-secretary.

MOXIE. I am afraid I couldn't possibly do that.

FELICITY. Why not?

MOXIE. I should feel so silly, Milady. Besides it wouldn't be right.

CRESTWELL. Now then, Dora, don't be stubborn.

MOXIE. This is my affair, Fred, and not yours. You've interfered enough already. We will have a little talk about it later when I can speak more freely.

FELICITY. You can speak perfectly freely here, Moxie.

MOXIE. Out of consideration for Crestwell I would rather not, Milady.

FELICITY. Why do you feel that it wouldn't be right for you to be my companion-secretary?

MOXIE. Well, I can't type for one thing, and my writing's terrible.

CRESTWELL. The question is one of status rather than actual achievement.

FELICITY (*anxiously*) That's the whole point.

MOXIE. You mean it would embarrass my sister less to find me in a false position rather than a real one?

PETER. *Touché!*

Moxie. Do you really think, Milady, that the position of a paid companion is so very superior to that of a paid lady's maid?

Felicity. Of course I don't, but in the eyes of the world I suppose it is.

Moxie. How would this—this change—if it took place—really help matters?

Felicity. Well, it would put you on a different footing in the house, Moxie. For instance you would take your meals with us, when we were alone. . . .

Moxie (*inexorably*) And when there were visitors?

Felicity (*floundering*) Well—I suppose that would really depend on how many there were—we thought of making the old Japanese room into a sort of private sitting-room for you—you could occasionally have a tray up there—in peace and quiet.

Moxie. I could even invite my sister up every now and then for a little snack, couldn't I, Milady?

Felicity. Don't be angry, Moxie. Please don't be angry.

Moxie. I'm not angry, Milady, really I'm not—and I understand what you're trying to do—but it's no good—it wouldn't work.

Felicity. Why are you so sure it wouldn't?

Moxie. Well, it stands to reason, doesn't it? I mean—it's me that's the trouble—I know I couldn't carry it off. You'd much better let me go, like I said, there isn't any other way out.

Peter. But even that isn't a way out. You'll still be Lord Marshwood's sister-in-law wherever you are.

Moxie. Nobody need ever know.

Felicity. Moxie, I won't accept such a sacrifice from you. If I did I should never forgive myself.

Moxie. Oh, Milady, don't take on so, you'll only start one of your headaches.

Peter. Do you absolutely refuse to consider her ladyship's suggestion? Even as a temporary measure, until we see how the land lies?

Moxie. It wouldn't do. It wouldn't be right.

Crestwell (*placing his hand on Moxie's arm*) Now look here, Dora. . . .

Moxie (*to Crestwell; savagely*) Unless you want to see me really lose my temper and make an exhibition of myself, you'll keep your tongue between your teeth.

Felicity. Oh, Moxie!

Moxie. I'm sorry, Milady, truly sorry, but the whole business is running me ragged and that's a fact. It's more than flesh and blood can stand. I haven't slept for three nights from worrying myself sick and trying to think what could be done. I don't want to leave this house, and you, any more than you want me to go. I've belonged here for nineteen years of my life and it's too late for me to try to start belonging anywhere else.

FELICITY. There's no question of you going away, Moxie. I want you to understand that clearly, once and for all.

MOXIE. I must, Milady. This idea of play-acting and pretending to be what I'm not won't settle anything. I'm what I am and I haven't got anything to be ashamed of.

CRESTWELL. We all know that, Dora, there's no sense in working yourself up.

MOXIE (*rising and crossing to* L *of the sofa; at bay*) And why shouldn't I work myself up? (*She moves up* C) God knows I've got enough reason for it. It's all very fine for you, Fred Crestwell, you're safe. You've got what you call a philosophical outlook and you never stop ramming it down all our throats until we're sick and tired of it. (*She moves to* L *of the sofa*) You're all right, you are. Nothing's going to knock you off your perch. (*She crosses to* L *of Crestwell*) I'm not saying you're not quite a good butler, too, as butlers go, even though you are a bit sloppy with the silver. (*She turns and moves down* LC)

CRESTWELL. May God forgive you for that, Dora.

MOXIE. No, I'm the one that's going to suffer over this, more than anybody, even more than you, Milady. I know it's awkward for you and puts you in an embarrassing position, but you don't stand to lose anything by it, not really. But if this marriage takes place I shan't have anything, neither my job nor my pride in it nor the feeling that I belong anywhere. I shall be mortified until the end of my days.

FELICITY (*distressed*) Oh, Moxie!

MOXIE (*crossing down* L; *near to tears*) I've always taken a pride in my work and done it to the best of my ability, and anybody who looks down on me for that can just get on with it. (*She moves to* R *of the desk and faces up stage*)

CRESTWELL (*rising and moving* R *of the sofa to* R *of Moxie; firmly*) Now see here, Dora. You just stop pitying yourself and use your loaf for a minute. Nobody's looking down on anybody. We all know you're a good worker, we all know you're upset and we all know why, so we needn't argue about that any more. We also know that your martyring yourself and going away won't solve anything, but something's got to be done, for her ladyship's sake as well as yours, and you've got to do it. There isn't much time and we've got to think fast.

MOXIE (*over her shoulder; angrily*) Don't you talk to me like that. . . .

CRESTWELL. Shut up a minute, Dora. (*To Felicity*) May I make a suggestion, Milady?

FELICITY. Of course you may. Keep calm, Moxie, Crestwell's right. (*To Crestwell*) What is it?

CRESTWELL (*taking charge*) Well. To begin with the secretary-companion idea won't wash for one very good reason.

PETER. What reason?

CRESTWELL. It isn't good enough.

MOXIE (*over her shoulder*) Oh, Fred—how can you say such a thing?

CRESTWELL. When Dora's sister arrives in this house she will naturally be received as one of the family, won't she?

FELICITY. Of course she will.

CRESTWELL. Then Dora will have to be, too.

PETER. I must say I see Crestwell's point.

FELICITY. So do I, but what I don't see is how it can possibly be arranged.

CRESTWELL. Just for a moment—begging your pardon, Milady.

(MOXIE *turns and stands above the left end of the sofa*)

FELICITY. Go on, Crestwell.

CRESTWELL. His lordship's been away now for over four months, hasn't he?

FELICITY. Yes.

CRESTWELL. Suppose that during that time an uncle of Dora's died in Australia and left her a large sum of money, enough to give her an income for life?

FELICITY. Yes—I'm beginning to see. Go on.

CRESTWELL. Being sentimentally attached to the family as you might say, she wouldn't want to leave Marshwood however financially independent she was, would she?

FELICITY. I don't know. Would you, Moxie?

MOXIE. Of course I wouldn't, Milady.

CRESTWELL (*triumphantly*) Therefore she would be staying on here—at least for the time being—as a personal friend, and meet her sister on equal terms, rather than as one of the staff.

FELICITY. Yes, I see that, but what I don't see is how this—could possibly be explained convincingly.

PETER. There isn't anyone to explain to, apart from Nigel. You can get him alone soon after he arrives and tell him about Moxie's uncle. You can add that she's very sensitive about having been a lady's maid and that he's not to say a word.

FELICITY. What about the Haylings?

PETER (*rising*) I'll deal with them. I'll pop over before dinner and tell them a little of the truth but not all of it, and swear them to secrecy.

FELICITY. Do you think you can do it, Moxie?

MOXIE (*moving down* LC) I don't like it, Milady—it doesn't feel right somehow—I don't like it at all.

FELICITY. Neither do I. But it's worth trying whether we like it or not.

MOXIE. Are you sure, Milady? Quite sure?

CRESTWELL. Come on, Dora, stop shilly-shallying.

MOXIE. Shut up, Fred, I'm talking to her ladyship. What about afterwards, Milady? (*She turns and moves above the sofa*)

FELICITY. Afterwards?

MOXIE. When they are married, I mean. Shall I have to go on staying here? In the house with her?

FELICITY (*helplessly*) I don't know. We shall have to decide that when the time comes. I shall probably go away, and if I do you will naturally come with me.

MOXIE. But not as a secretary-companion, or a friend of the family's, or your son's sister-in-law, only as your maid, like I've always been.

FELICITY (*rising and crossing to* R *of Moxie*) Very well, Moxie, that's a promise.

(CRESTWELL *moves down* R)

MOXIE. All right then, Milady—I'll do it, if you think I can. I'll do my best anyway.

FELICITY (*crossing below Moxie to* L *of her*) Do you think she'll recognize you?

MOXIE. I don't know, she hasn't laid eyes on me for twenty years. I've been saving a few things to say to that one even if she does recognize me or not. I can forgive her for running off and leaving me alone with Mum on my hands, and never a word from her from that day to this, but what I can't forgive her for is coming back and shoving her nose in where she doesn't belong.

PETER. Do you hate her, Moxie?

MOXIE. Of course I don't. She's not worth it. She was always an affected little piece and out for what she could get. If ever a girl needed her bottom smacking she did.

PETER. We might arrange that after dinner.

FELICITY. Shhh! Peter. You'd better wear my Molyneux this evening. We'll discuss other clothes in the morning.

MOXIE. I'll bring your tea in half an hour early.

FELICITY. I think Mr Peter has some idea about your hair. You'd better listen to him, he's quite good at that sort of thing.

MOXIE. Very good, Milady. (*To Peter*) Thank you, sir.

FELICITY (*crossing below Moxie to* RC) I think Moxie had better have the chintz room, Crestwell. You might see that her things are moved, will you?

CRESTWELL. Very good, Milady. I gather, to coin a phrase, that we're off. (*He moves to the hall doors*)

FELICITY. We certainly are. Go along, Moxie.

(*The sound of a car horn is heard off. They all turn and look towards the french windows*)

(*She crosses quickly to the alcove and looks off* L) Good heavens, they're arriving. Fly, Moxie—quickly.

Moxie (*running to Felicity and holding her hand; giggling*) Oh, Milady—I don't think I can—I really don't.

Felicity. Courage, Moxie.

(Moxie *turns, crosses to* L *of Crestwell, suddenly draws herself up and speaks in a changed voice*)

Moxie. Crestwell, tell Alice to run me a bath, will you, please?

(Felicity *claps her hands and moves above the sofa.* Moxie *turns to Felicity and smiles*)

Crestwell (*smiling and bowing obsequiously*) Very good, Mrs Moxton.

Moxie (*to Crestwell*) And you might wipe that grin off your face while you're at it.

Moxie *makes a dignified exit to the hall, and* Felicity *moves joyfully to Peter as—*

the Curtain *falls*

ACT II

Scene i

Scene—*The same. Two hours later. Before dinner.*

When the Curtain *rises* Felicity *is seated on the sofa, at the right end of it, knitting. She wears a dinner gown.* Nigel, *the Earl of Marshwood, stands with his back to the fireplace. He is aged about thirty-five. He is good-looking and has charm. There is perhaps a little weakness about him, a suggestion of petulance, but one feels that, on the whole, he is a pleasant fellow. At the moment he is slightly irritable. He wears dinner clothes.*

Nigel. But I still don't quite understand, Mother.

Felicity. I should have thought it was simple enough.

Nigel. I'm fond of Moxie, as you know. I always have been. But I can't help feeling that this—this sudden transformation is a little drastic.

Felicity. It's her way of starting a new life, you know, like people going off to Rhodesia.

Nigel. It would be a damned sight less awkward if she had gone to Rhodesia.

Felicity. Not for me, dear. I can't bear wide open spaces. They give me whatever's the opposite of claustrophobia.

Nigel. Is it absolutely necessary for you to go wherever she goes, to be clamped to her side, for the rest of your days?

Felicity. Absolutely. I'm devoted to her and she's devoted to me.

Nigel (*moving below the right end of the sofa*) But surely, if she's financially independent and no longer your maid, you can't expect her to fetch and carry for you and look after you.

Felicity. Moxie would continue to look after me if she were a millionairess.

Nigel (*crossing below the sofa to* l) If you ask me I think the whole thing is absurd. (*He turns*) You don't want to be known as an eccentric, do you?

Felicity. I wouldn't really mind. Eccentrics have a lovely time. Look at old Maud Nethersole, she's merry as a grig from morning till night.

Nigel. Old Maud Nethersole's not an eccentric, she's plain dotty. (*He crosses to the table down* l *and pours a drink for himself*)

Felicity. I still don't see why you're making such a dreadful fuss. Moxie's been with us for years, she's part of the family. Why shouldn't she have meals with us and call us by our christian names?

NIGEL. Why shouldn't she! Really, Mother!

FELICITY. Well, give me one valid reason.

NIGEL. To begin with it's unsuitable. (*He picks up his glass and crosses to* L *of the sofa*) It's also extremely embarrassing. You must see that.

FELICITY. Sylvia Fowler calls us by our christian names, in fact she positively deafens us with them.

NIGEL. That's quite different. She's Jack Fowler's wife and we've known him all our lives.

FELICITY. She was a manicurist at Selfridges.

NIGEL. Harrods. (*He drinks*)

FELICITY. She's a perfect horror, anyhow, and she has no neck into the bargain.

NIGEL (*crossing above the sofa to the fireplace*) If her head were sunk between her shoulders it still wouldn't have any bearing on what we're talking about.

FELICITY. Oh yes, it would. And it does. Why should you be willing to accept on equal terms a loud-voiced vulgarian with no neck, and turn up your nose at poor darling Moxie who has devoted the best years of her life to us?

NIGEL (*moving down* R) I'm not turning up my nose at her, but I still think it would be uncomfortable for her and for us to have her lolling about the house all day long, knocking back Dry Martinis.

FELICITY. You make your ancestral home sound like *Great Fosters*.

NIGEL. What's Aunt Rose going to say?

FELICITY. Aunt Rose is in too much of a frizz about your marrying a film star to worry her head about Moxie.

NIGEL. How dare she be in a frizz? It's none of her damned business.

FELICITY. Neither's this.

NIGEL. Miranda's one of the most wonderful people in the world. She's given romance and happiness to millions.

FELICITY. With the apparent exception of Aunt Rose.

NIGEL. To hell with Aunt Rose! (*He puts his glass on the table below the fireplace*)

FELICITY. Will you do as I ask? About Moxie I mean?

NIGEL. I suppose so. (*Moving down* R *below the tub chair*). But I don't approve of it and I never shall.

FELICITY. And you'll promise not to tell anyone, even Miranda?

NIGEL. How can you be so silly, Mother? Everybody's bound to know sooner or later.

FELICITY. Will you promise?

NIGEL. If you insist.

FELICITY. I do insist. It's terribly important.

NIGEL. All right, I promise.

FELICITY. After all it won't be for long. We shall be going away soon.

NIGEL. Why should you? (*He wanders up* R)

FELICITY. Because this is your home, darling, and I presume that you and Miranda will wish to live in it.

NIGEL (*moving to the fireplace*) It's your home, too.

FELICITY. Only for as long as you are unattached, dear. Mothers-in-law can be horribly tedious. It wouldn't be fair to Miranda.

NIGEL. You got along with Joan all right.

FELICITY. Getting along with Joan all right was one of the most spectacular achievements of my whole life. My nervous system has never quite recovered from it.

NIGEL (*moving down* R; *reminiscently*) Poor old Joan, she certainly was a crashing bore, wasn't she? I can't think why I ever married her.

FELICITY. I used to ponder that question myself sometimes, when she was playing the piano.

NIGEL. She thumped a bit but she wasn't all that bad.

FELICITY. We had to have it re-felted after the divorce.

NIGEL (*crossing and sitting* L *of Felicity on the sofa*) Do you like Miranda, Mother—really?

FELICITY. I only had a few words with her and then she said she wanted to go to sleep.

NIGEL. She was exhausted after the drive down. She always sleeps in the afternoon anyhow.

FELICITY. How sensible.

NIGEL (*persistently*) Do you think you are going to like her?

FELICITY. I hope so, darling. She seemed very charming. Of course she has no eyebrows.

NIGEL. Your mind seems to be running on anatomical defects this evening.

FELICITY. I didn't say it was a defect. I merely said that she hadn't got any.

NIGEL. She's awfully simple and sweet really, you know. Quite unlike what you'd think she'd be from seeing her on the screen.

FELICITY. I've only seen her as a hospital nurse, a gangster's moll, a nun, and Catherine the Great, so it's a little difficult to form any definite opinion.

NIGEL. I'm very much in love with her.

FELICITY. I'm sure you are, dear.

NIGEL. I suppose it was a great shock to you, wasn't it?

FELICITY. I think it would have been more considerate if you had prepared the ground a little beforehand.

NIGEL. It all happened so quickly.

FELICITY. What did, dear?

NIGEL. Well, meeting her and falling in love with her and asking her to marry me. It was extraordinary, really it was, like a sudden flash of light.

Felicity. She must have been used to that, having been photographed so much I mean.

Nigel. It all happened at Cap d'Antibes. We found ourselves alone together on a raft . . .

Felicity. Like the Kon Tiki expedition.

Nigel. And we both knew somehow, in the first glance, that we were made for each other.

Felicity. There can have been very little to prevent you.

Nigel. I suppose all this laboured flippancy is merely to cover up what you really feel?

Felicity. I don't know what I really feel yet. I haven't had time to find out.

Nigel. You're prejudiced against her. That's fairly obvious at any rate.

Felicity. What did you expect me to be?

Nigel. A little more sympathetic. I know it's all very sudden, and that I should have given you more warning, but you might have a little confidence in my taste and judgement.

Felicity. Your love life since the age of eighteen, darling, has been a trifle too erratic to inspire confidence in either your taste or your judgement.

Nigel. That's not Miranda's fault. You haven't got to know her yet. You might at least give her the benefit of the doubt.

Felicity (*sweetly*) I do, dear. I give her the benefit of very grave doubts.

Nigel. Well, all I can say is, it's damned unfair of you.

Felicity (*firmly*) Don't talk nonsense, Nigel. I'm not being in the least unfair. As your mother it's perfectly natural that I should be prejudiced against the idea of Miranda Frayle becoming my daughter-in-law. I know nothing whatever about her personal habits beyond the fact that she sleeps every afternoon and can swim.

Nigel. She's a remarkable character. She's honest and unaffected and she's never allowed her success to spoil her; she hates show-off and display, she loves the ordinary, simple things of life, like living in the country and sewing and reading. She also adores children.

Felicity. Has she ever had any?

Nigel. No, she hasn't. But that's beside the point.

Felicity. She's been married before, hasn't she?

Nigel. Yes, to a man called Greenberg. He was foul to her.

Felicity. In what way?

Nigel. In every way. He was cruel, and used to go away and leave her alone for weeks at a time.

Felicity. That at least gave her an opportunity to catch up on her sewing and reading.

NIGEL (*rising, moving to the alcove steps* L *and gazing out of the window*) It's quite clear that you've hardened your heart against her so I won't say any more.

FELICITY (*after a slight pause*) I saw in the paper that Mr Don Lucas has arrived in England.

NIGEL (*turning and moving down* C) What are you getting at now, Mother?

FELICITY. Mightn't that be a little awkward for Miranda?

NIGEL. Do you suppose I don't know about Don Lucas and Miranda?

FELICITY. No, dear. Their rather convulsive relationship practically comes under the heading of General Information. I merely thought that it was unfortunate that he should arrive just now. After all, it is assumed by the world at large that he is the love of her life.

NIGEL. As I told you before, Mother, Miranda is completely honest. She's never attempted to conceal anything from me. I know all about her love affair with Don Lucas. It was finished and done with ages ago; three-quarters of it was studio publicity, anyway.

FELICITY. I'm so glad, darling.

NIGEL. It's unwise to believe what you read in the papers.

FELICITY. I know. Everyone says that, but somehow one always does.

NIGEL. Studio publicity agents are absolutely unscrupulous. Their job is to get the stars talked about at all costs. Miranda and Don Lucas were teamed together in three pictures. That was quite enough to start the whole business. (*He moves to* R *of the chair down* L)

FELICITY. I remember him in the one about the nun. He was very good.

NIGEL. He's a terrible drunk, you know.

FELICITY. How horrid for her. When do you intend to get married?

NIGEL. As soon as possible.

FELICITY. I see. Has she any family? Any relations?

NIGEL (*moving to* L *of the sofa*) Her mother died when she was eighteen, she was terribly cut up about it, that's one of the reasons she went to America.

FELICITY. What were the others?

NIGEL. She had to earn her living. She was a professional dancer.

FELICITY. Acrobatic or ballroom?

NIGEL (*crossing to the table* R) I don't know, Mother. Does it matter? (*He picks up his glass*)

FELICITY. Of course it doesn't matter. It wouldn't matter if she'd spent her early years upside down on a trapeze. I'm merely eager to find out as much as possible about her background. Has she any brothers or sisters?

NIGEL (*moving below the right end of the sofa; reluctantly*) There was a sister, I believe. A good deal older than she was. Miranda doesn't like to talk about her much.

FELICITY. Why not?

NIGEL. Apparently she went to the bad.

FELICITY. In any specific way or just generally?

NIGEL. I'm not sure. All I know is that poor Miranda helped her as much as she could.

FELICITY. How?

NIGEL. Oh, she was constantly sending her money, but it was no good, it all went on drink. (*He drinks*)

FELICITY (*rising and moving down* LC) Poor Miranda. She does seem to be haunted by intemperance, doesn't she? (*She turns*) Is she still alive, the sister?

NIGEL. No, I don't think so.

FELICITY. Just as well. She might have turned up at the wedding and started throwing bottles at everybody. (*She moves to the table in the alcove and puts her knitting into the work-box*)

NIGEL (*crossing to the table down* L) Miranda hasn't had a particularly easy life. I expect that's why she wants to get away from it all and settle down. (*He puts his glass on the table*)

FELICITY (*crossing to* L *of the sofa*) I expect it is. The English peerage has often proved a convenient shelter for the world weary.

NIGEL (*moving below the chair down* L) Now you're being sarcastic.

FELICITY. I don't seem to be able to put a foot right this evening. It's very discouraging.

NIGEL (*pointing to the table down* L) Why hasn't Crestwell brought in the cocktail things?

FELICITY. I'll ring. (*She crosses to the fireplace and rings the bell*) We're rather short-handed at the moment. May has shingles you know.

NIGEL. Good God! Are they catching?

FELICITY (*moving to* R *of the sofa*) I don't think so. But in any case you weren't planning to spend much of your time with her, were you?

(PETER *enters from the hall, and moves to* R *of the table above the sofa. He wears dinner clothes*)

PETER. Felicity, there are two Girl Guides in the shrubbery. I saw them from my window.

FELICITY. What were they doing?

PETER. They weren't doing anything. (*He moves to* L *of the sofa*) They were just there.

NIGEL. If they're autograph hunters they must be sent away. Miranda is driven mad by autograph hunters.

FELICITY. Poor dear.

(PETER *sits on the sofa at the left end.*

CRESTWELL *enters from the hall. He carries a tray with a cocktail shaker, a long spoon, and a container of lemon peel.*

ALICE *follows him on. She carries an ice bucket with ice and tongs.* NIGEL *sits in the chair down* L. CRESTWELL *crosses above the sofa towards the alcove*)

(*She moves above the sofa*) There are apparently some Girl Guides in the shrubbery, Crestwell.

CRESTWELL. I know, Milady. They've been hanging about all the afternoon. I think one of them is the little Mumby girl. (*He crosses to the table down* L *and puts the tray on it*)

NIGEL. Have them sent away whoever they are.

FELICITY (*moving down* R) If it's Elsie Mumby we can't possibly send her away. The whole village would be up in arms.

NIGEL. Why?

FELICITY (*moving to the fireplace and taking a cigarette from the box on the mantelpiece*) She pulled her little brother out of a well. She's a local heroine. (*She lights her cigarette*)

CRESTWELL. Put the ice bucket down, Alice, and go and see what they want.

ALICE (*crossing down* L) They want Miss Frayle's autograph, Mr Crestwell. (*She puts the ice bucket on the table down* L) So does Miss Luton at the post office. She sent Billy down for it on his bike.

CRESTWELL. Collect their books from them, Alice, and tell them to call for them in the morning.

(FELICITY *moves down* R)

ALICE. Yes, Mr Crestwell.

CRESTWELL. And don't stand about giggling with them either.

ALICE. No, Mr Crestwell.

(ALICE *exits by the french windows*)

FELICITY (*sitting in the chair* R) Thank you, Crestwell. I expect we shall have quite a lot of this sort of thing to deal with.

CRESTWELL (*crossing below the sofa to* R) There's the question of press reporters also, Milady. I would like to have instructions as to what to say to them.

(FELICITY *puts the lighter on Crestwell's tray*)

NIGEL. Get rid of them.

CRESTWELL. Young Willis of the *Kentish Times* has been particularly insistent, My Lord. He's rung up seven times and called twice. (*He puts the lighter on the table* R).

NIGEL. Tell him to go to hell.

FELICITY. Don't be silly, Nigel. We can't possibly tell old Mrs Willis's son to go to hell. She's one of my staunchest supporters on the Cottage Hospital Committee, and she made us all those wool mats for the sale of work.

CRESTWELL. If, My Lord, you could spare him a few moments of your time tomorrow and perhaps present him briefly to Miss Miranda Frayle, it would mean a great deal to him. He's an ambitious lad and worthy of encouragement.

NIGEL. One of the reasons that I brought Miss Frayle here, Crestwell, was to protect her from newspaper men and autograph hunters and all the other pests who badger the life out of her.

FELICITY (*firmly*) You'll have to see young Willis, Nigel, and so will she. He was splendid during the election and always gives us a half page every year for the church fête. (*To Crestwell*) Tell young Willis to come and see me tomorrow morning.

CRESTWELL. Very good, Milady.

(CRESTWELL *exits to the hall, closing the doors behind him*)

NIGEL (*rising and moving up* LC) Really, Mother. I do think it's very inconsiderate of you.

FELICITY. Nonsense, dear. If Miranda has decided to come and live in a small English village, she must be prepared for publicity. Will you make the cocktails or shall I?

PETER. You please, Nigel. Felicity never puts enough gin in.

NIGEL (*crossing to the table down* L) All right. Martini for everybody? (*He fills the shaker and mixes the cocktail*)

FELICITY. Yes please, dear.

PETER (*rising and moving up* L *of the sofa*) It's quite a festive occasion, isn't it? What with one thing and another.

(MIRANDA FRAYLE *enters from the hall, opening both doors as she does so. Her appearance is impeccable. She wears a simple dinner dress and her jewellery is discreet. She carries a large chintz work bag*)

FELICITY. Ah, there you are, Miranda. I do hope you had a good rest.

MIRANDA (*moving above the sofa; simply*) I went to sleep in one world and woke up in another.

FELICITY. How confusing.

MIRANDA. I was tired and edgy after the drive down, and nervous too, about meeting you and Nigel's friends, and wondering what you would all think of me. But when I woke up everything was different. I felt smooth and peaceful for the first time in weeks. Perhaps it was the room. What a lovely, lovely room it is. Is it haunted?

FELICITY. That rather depends on who occupies it.

PETER (*leaning on the downstage pillar of the alcove*) When Judy Lavenham had it it used to be known as Victoria Station.

NIGEL. Shut up, Peter.

FELICITY (*to Miranda*) Come and sit down, my dear.

MIRANDA (*moving below the sofa*) I've brought my work. (*She sits on the sofa at the right end*) I hope nobody minds.

FELICITY. Not in the least. Why should they?

NIGEL (*to Miranda*) Martini, darling?

MIRANDA. No, thank you, dear. I'd like a soft drink if there is one.

NIGEL (*pouring a drink for Miranda*) Lemon juice with a little soda?

MIRANDA. Perfect. (*To Felicity*) I want to keep my mind absolutely clear and let every new impression sink in. You know what I mean, don't you? I want to let the atmosphere sort of take charge of me.

(NIGEL *crosses to Miranda and gives her the drink*)

NIGEL (*crossing to the table down* L) Peter, come and help.

FELICITY. I didn't think you'd want to meet many strangers on your first evening here, so, apart from us there will only be Admiral and Lady Hayling dining. They are very old friends and our closest neighbours.

(NIGEL *pours three cocktails*)

MIRANDA. Is there anyone else staying in the house?

FELICITY. Only Peter and—and Moxie. (*She glances at Nigel*)

MIRANDA (*sipping her drink*) Is that a nickname?

FELICITY. Yes, I suppose it is. Her name is Mrs Moxton. We've known her for so many years that she is practically one of the family. Isn't she, Nigel?

MIRANDA. I do hope she'll approve of me.

(NIGEL, *faintly irritated by Miranda's humility, crosses to Felicity and hands her a cocktail*)

NIGEL. Why the hell shouldn't she? (*He crosses to the table down* L)

MIRANDA. Old family friends are liable to resent intruders even more than the family itself.

(MOXIE *enters from the hall. She is dressed in a plain dinner dress. Her hair is becomingly done. She wears two strings of pearls and an obviously expensive bracelet on her right wrist. She wears large horn-rimmed spectacles.* MIRANDA *puts her glass on the table* R *of the sofa*)

MOXIE (*standing in the open doorway*) I hope I'm not late?

FELICITY. Of course not, Moxie, dear.

NIGEL (*with an effort*) Hello, Moxie.

MOXIE (*crossing to Nigel and shaking hands with him*) Welcome home, my . . . My goodness, how well you look.

(CRESTWELL *appears in the hall and closes the doors*)

FELICITY (*hurriedly*) Miss Miranda Frayle—Mrs Moxton.

(MOXIE *crosses to* L *of Miranda*)

MIRANDA. How do you do? I've heard so much about you. I do really hope that we are going to be friends.

MOXIE. I feel I already know you well, Miss Frayle.

MIRANDA (*with charming impulsiveness*) Won't you call me Miranda?

MOXIE. Certainly. (*She sits* L *of Miranda on the sofa*) I should adore to.

MIRANDA (*sincerely*) Thank you for that. Thank you a great deal. I know how difficult this must be for you—for all of you. After all, you none of you know what I'm really like. You have to judge by appearances. And appearances can be deceptive, can't they? (*She takes some needlework and her spectacles from the work bag*)

FELICITY. Yes, fortunately. Think how uncomfortable life would be if we knew all about each other at the first glance.

MOXIE (*taking her handkerchief from her bag*) This is a great moment, I am one of your most ardent fans. (*She uses her handkerchief*)

MIRANDA (*graciously*) Thank you.

MOXIE. Peter, be an angel and get me a drink. I'm positively gasping.

NIGEL (*wincing, but recovering himself*) I presume you do want a Martini, Moxie?

MOXIE. Yes, please, my—my dear.

(NIGEL *pours a cocktail for Moxie*)

MIRANDA (*ostentatiously putting on the spectacles*) You've no idea how wonderful it is to be able to relax and pop on my old glasses and not worry what I look like.

NIGEL. As a matter of fact they're very becoming.

MIRANDA (*blowing a kiss to Nigel*) Thank you, sweet.

(PETER *moves to the table down* L, *picks up two cocktails and takes one to Moxie*)

PETER. Are you a keen needlewoman, Miss Frayle?

MIRANDA (*threading a needle*) Yes. I always have been.

(NIGEL *picks up his cocktail.* PETER *moves above the sofa*)

Ever since I was a child. I used to have to do most of the sewing and mending at home. We were terribly poor, you know. (*She sews*) I remember mother was always calling me in from playing in the street, to darn stockings, or put a hem on something or other. We couldn't afford a machine.

MOXIE. Playing in the street?

(PETER *crosses and stands up* L *of Felicity.* NIGEL *sits in the chair down* L)

MIRANDA (*with a gay laugh*) Oh yes. I was a regular little gutter child. One of my earliest memories was making a doll's house out of an old cardboard box I found in the dustbin.

MOXIE. Where did you live?

MIRANDA (*looking at Moxie*) Oh, it was an awful slum, really—not far from the Brixton High Street.

MOXIE (*with iron control*) An awful slum? (*She laughs nervously then sips her drink*)

MIRANDA (*reminiscently*) Oh yes. I can see it now—on a Saturday night with the crowds and the lights. I used to go and get mother her pint of beer at the pub and bring it home in a jug. One night there was a barrel organ and I danced to it.

MOXIE. How old were you?

MIRANDA. Oh, about five, I suppose.

MOXIE. You danced to a barrel organ outside a pub when you were five?

MIRANDA (*smiling wistfully*) Oh yes. That's how I first learnt to dance really. (*To Felicity*) I do hope these sordid disclosures about my childhood aren't shocking you?

NIGEL. Don't be silly, darling, of course they're not.

FELICITY. On the contrary, I find them absolutely fascinating, don't you, Moxie?

MOXIE. I certainly do. (*She drinks*)

MIRANDA. I was born in the gutter, within the sound of Bow bells. I'm a London Cockney and I'm proud of it.

FELICITY. I'm sure you are. It must be lovely.

MIRANDA. Yesterday, without even telling Nigel, I put on some old clothes and a veil and went in a tram to Brixton—all by myself. (*She puts her sewing beside her on the sofa*)

MOXIE. How did it look—the slum? (*She drinks*)

MIRANDA (*gazing out front*) Changed very much. Twenty years is a long time. The house was still there though. It gave me a dreadful pang to see the window of mother's room, the one she died in.

MOXIE. I expect you nursed her devotedly, didn't you?

MIRANDA (*simply*) I did the best I could, but it wasn't much.

PETER (*moving down* R *of the sofa*) And you were all alone? With no father or brother or sister?

MIRANDA (*picking up her drink*) My father died soon after I was born. (*She sips her drink*) I did have one sister, she was a good deal older than me—poor old Dora. (*She puts her glass on the table* R *of the sofa*)

PETER. Why—what happened to her?

MIRANDA. Oh—what always happens to people when they allow life to get the better of them.

FELICITY. In what way did life get the better of her?

MIRANDA (*removing her spectacles*) In every way, really. You see she sort of started off on the wrong foot. I was the lucky one. I always had a conviction, deep down inside me, that somehow or other I should get on, hoist myself up out of the mire, escape from the poverty and squalor of my surroundings. I suppose I must have been born with the will to succeed.

(Moxie *takes a cigarette from the box on the table* L *of the sofa, nervously taps the cigarette on her hand, then picks up the lighter*)

That's what's so unfair, isn't it? I mean that some people should feel like that from the very beginning and that other people shouldn't.

(Moxie *lights her cigarette*)

I think that's why Dora hated me really. Because I had so much and she had so little.

Peter. Was she cruel to you?

Miranda. Oh no. Not exactly cruel, she just didn't understand me.

Peter. She never actually ill-treated you? She never beat you or knocked you about?

Miranda (*replacing her spectacles in the bag*) Never, when she was sober.

Moxie (*firmly*) I think I'd like another dry Martini, please.

(Miranda *puts her sewing into the bag.* Peter *collects Felicity's empty glass, crosses above the sofa and picks up Moxie's glass*)

Peter. I expect we all would. (*He crosses to the table down* L *and refills the glasses*)

Felicity. You haven't told us yet what happened to her. Is she still alive?

Miranda. No. She died some years ago. (*She picks up her drink*) The news came to me in quite a roundabout way. I hadn't heard from her for ages. I'd been sending her pennies every now and then, you know, just to help out, and food parcels and things like that, but she never acknowledged them. I'm afraid the pennies all went on drink. (*She drinks*)

Peter. I expect the food parcels came in handy as blotting paper.

Miranda. Then when I heard that she had died in horrid, sordid circumstances, it really upset me more than I could ever have believed possible. I had to go to Palm Springs, to sort of get myself straight with myself.

Felicity. Palm Springs sounds heavenly, doesn't it? Almost biblical.

Miranda. You see, I suddenly realized that for the first time in my life, I had failed, failed utterly. I felt guilty and ashamed, as though it was all my fault, my responsibility. Of course it wasn't really, I suppose—but you know how silly one is about that kind of thing. (*She drinks*)

FELICITY. Indeed I do.

(MOXIE *and* NIGEL *look at Felicity*)

Both my sisters are fairly heavy drinkers. Of course, they're still alive, but I never see a telegram come into the house without saying to myself, "Caroline's gone too far at last", or, "Sarah's had it!" (*She stubs out her cigarette in the ashtray on the table below the fireplace*)

(NIGEL *rises and crosses to the table down* L. PETER *picks up two drinks, crosses and hands one to Moxie and one to Felicity*)

PETER. Here's your drink, Moxie. Felicity.

FELICITY. It looks very pale, dear. After all, the vermouth is there to be used, you know.

PETER (*to Miranda; amiably*) I think it only right and proper that you should be warned about your future mother-in-law. She's famous for her meanness over inessentials.

FELICITY. I wouldn't call gin an inessential.

PETER. Of course over the major issues she's generous to a fault. Why, she'd give you the dress off her back, wouldn't she, Moxie?

MOXIE. Certainly she would, Mr . . . Mr—Mr Bagshot was saying so only the other day.

PETER (*wickedly*) Who is Mr Bagshot?

(MOXIE *drinks*)

FELICITY (*hitting Peter's leg*) Mr Bagshot is the new curate, Peter.

NIGEL (*moving down* LC) New curate. What's happened to Eustace Parker, then? Has he left?

FELICITY. Yes, dear—under a cloud.

NIGEL. You never said anything about it in your letters.

(PETER *turns to Felicity, in fits of laughter*)

FELICITY. I couldn't, darling. There are some things you just can't put in letters.

NIGEL. But he was such a mild, inoffensive little chap. What on earth did he do?

FELICITY. We have no proof that he actually did anything. It—it was just one of those things.

NIGEL. One of what things?

PETER. One of those crazy things.

FELICITY. I'll tell you all about it later, Nigel. I really would rather not go on about it now. Miranda, dear, surely it's time you had a proper drink? That lemonade looks so dreary.

MIRANDA. No, thank you, I hardly ever do, you know. Funnily enough it's Hollywood that taught me not to drink. And one sort of gets into the habit of disciplining oneself. (*She puts her glass on the table above the sofa*)

PETER. I hope, for all our sakes, for the sake of the world at large, that you haven't decided to give up acting for good.

MIRANDA. I'm afraid I have. (*She smiles at Nigel, rises and crosses to him with outstretched arms*) I think being married to Pete will be a whole time job. (*She holds Nigel's hand*)

FELICITY. Pete?

MIRANDA (*with a laugh*) Oh dear, it slipped out. I always call him Pete, it's a sort of silly habit. He calls me Pete, too, sometimes.

(NIGEL *puts his arm around Miranda*)

FELICITY. Isn't that rather muddling?

MIRANDA (*to Nigel*) We manage to understand each other, don't we, darling?

NIGEL. It's Miranda's idea that she should give up her career. Personally, I think she owes it to the public to make one picture a year at least, but she won't hear of it. (*He kisses Miranda on the cheek*)

PETER. Why not?

MIRANDA (*breaking from Nigel and crossing to* C) Don't you see? Don't you really see? (*Impressively*) It's just that I love Nigel. I love him with all my heart, and I'm absolutely determined that the Countess of Marshwood shall be the longest and the greatest part I ever played.

FELICITY. I hope you won't find it too much of a strain.

NIGEL. Mother!

FELICITY. I know what I'm talking about. I played it for years. Nigel's dear father was my leading man. I found it a good part but technically rather exhausting.

(MIRANDA *and* NIGEL *move down* L.

CRESTWELL *enters from the hall, opening both doors as he does so*)

CRESTWELL (*standing* L *of the doors; announcing*) Admiral Sir John and Lady Hayling.

PETER (*to Felicity; in an agonized whisper*) My God! I forgot to warn them. (*He stands above Felicity and faces the fireplace*)

(FELICITY *rises, puts her glass on the table* R *of the sofa and faces the hall doors.* MOXIE *rises and moves to* L *of Felicity.*

LADY HAYLING *and the* ADMIRAL *enter from the hall.* LADY HAYLING *moves to Felicity. The* ADMIRAL *crosses and stands* R *of the desk.*

CRESTWELL *exits to the hall, closing the doors behind him*)

LADY HAYLING. I'm sorry we're late, Felicity. Poor Eustace Parker arrived just as we were leaving . . .

NIGEL (*crossing to* LC) Eustace Parker?

FELICITY (*hurriedly*) Oh, I'm so glad he's back. It must all have blown over.

LADY HAYLING. What are you talking about, Felicity?

FELICITY. Nothing, dear. I'll tell you all about it later.

ADMIRAL (*moving to Nigel and shaking hands with him*) Hello, Nigel. (*He stands* L *of Nigel*)

LADY HAYLING (*crossing above the sofa to Nigel*) Welcome home, my dear. (*She kisses him*)

FELICITY. Cynthia, John—this is Miranda. Miranda Frayle.

ADMIRAL (*turning to Miranda; gruffly*) How do you do?

LADY HAYLING (*crossing to Miranda and shaking hands with her*) We've so often admired you—from afar.

MIRANDA. Thank you.

LADY HAYLING (*turning and seeing Moxie*) Moxie! You look very dressy. If you have time while we're at dinner, you might be a dear and put a few stitches in my bag; I meant to ask Saunders to do it before I left the house, but I forgot.

MOXIE (*after a slight pause*) Really, Cynthia—you'll be forgetting your head next. (*She crosses above Felicity and stands above the fireplace*)

(MIRANDA *sits in the chair down* L. NIGEL *crosses and stands* R *of her*)

LADY HAYLING (*crossing below the sofa; scandalized*) What did you say?

FELICITY (*moving quickly to Lady Hayling and taking her by the arm*) Cynthia—(*she puts her other hand on the Admiral's arm*) John, too—I simply must talk to you both about the Cottage Hospital. There's the most awful crisis on about the matron. I'm at my wit's end. She really has gone too far this time. (*She leads them down* R) Come into the study. I can't talk about it in front of everyone, and you're both so sane about that sort of thing—please come. Make another cocktail, Peter, we shan't be a minute.

(NIGEL *crosses towards Felicity*)

No, not you, Nigel, nothing whatever to do with you.

(FELICITY *propels* LADY HAYLING *and the* ADMIRAL *off down* R, *follows them off and closes the door behind her*)

NIGEL. What on earth's the matter with mother this evening? She's quite hysterical.

PETER (*moving down* R) That matron is enough to make anyone hysterical. She's a fiend incarnate.

NIGEL. If you're referring to Mrs Gaskin, Peter, she is adored by the whole district.

PETER. This isn't Mrs Gaskin. It's a new one.

NIGEL. Since when?

PETER. Since Mrs Gaskin died, of course.

NIGEL. I never knew the poor old girl had died. When did it happen?

PETER. About three weeks ago, I believe.

NIGEL. What did she die of?

PETER (*crossing to the table down* L) It's no good cross-questioning me. (*He mixes a fresh cocktail and fills the glasses*) I wasn't here. Anyhow I feel sure that all these local incidents cannot be of the faintest interest to Miranda.

MIRANDA. But of course they are. They're part of my new life. I want to know everything. I want to learn step by step, all about this funny, dear English world that's going to be my home. It's terribly important to me. It is really.

NIGEL. Darling.

(MOXIE *moves to the table* R *of the sofa and stubs out her cigarette in the ashtray*)

MIRANDA (*rising and moving to* L *of Nigel; affectionately*) I don't suppose it will be easy just at first, in the village I mean, getting the people to trust me, to look upon me as a friend, but I'll win them round in the long run. Just you see.

(FELICITY, LADY HAYLING *and the* ADMIRAL *enter down* R. FELICITY *moves down* RC.

CRESTWELL *enters from the hall, opening both doors as he does so*)

CRESTWELL (*standing* L *of the doors; announcing*) Dinner is served, My Lord.

FELICITY (*to the Admiral*) Oh dear—and I snatched you away before you'd even had a cocktail.

LADY HAYLING. We can take them in with us.

FELICITY. I think that would be the best if you really don't mind. We're starting with a soufflé.

(*The* ADMIRAL *and* LADY HAYLING *move up* R)

PETER (*picking up two drinks*) I'll carry them for you.

(MIRANDA *and* NIGEL *cross above the sofa to the hall door.* PETER *crosses to the Admiral and Lady Hayling and hands them their drinks.*

MIRANDA *and* NIGEL *exit to the hall.* LADY HAYLING, *the* ADMIRAL *and* PETER *follow them off, all chatting cheerfully*)

MOXIE (*to Felicity; muttering*) Please go on, I'll see you later.

(FELICITY *exits to the hall.* MOXIE, *until the others are out of sight, makes a pretence of looking for her bag on the sofa. She then removes her spectacles and sinks down on to the sofa*)

CRESTWELL. Dora.

MOXIE. I can't do it—I know I can't.

CRESTWELL (*crossing to* L *of the sofa*) Pull yourself together.

MOXIE. I can't sit and listen to her talking about mum like

that, saying she took her jugs of beer from pubs. Mum never touched a drop in her life. She was a respectable, God-fearing woman from the day she was born until the day she died.

CRESTWELL. Come off it, Dora. She can't have been all that God-fearing the day she was born.

MOXIE. You think it's very funny, don't you?

CRESTWELL. I cannot truthfully deny that, to me, there is a certain whimsical humour in the whole curious lash-up.

MOXIE (*rising and crossing to* R *of Crestwell*) You didn't hear her. You didn't hear the black lies she told. . . .

CRESTWELL. There you wrong me, Dora. I contrived to acquaint myself with most of the salient points of your sister's discourse by the simple device of clamping my ear to the keyhole.

MOXIE. I'll never forgive her. Never, never, never.

CRESTWELL. Come along now. They'll be wondering what's happened to you.

MOXIE (*putting her hand to her head; near to tears*) Oh, Fred. . . .

CRESTWELL. Now, now—none of that. (*He crosses to the table down* L, *picks up a half-filled glass of dry Martini and takes it to Moxie*) Here—knock this back.

MOXIE. No—I'd better not—really.

CRESTWELL. Drink it. It won't hurt an old soak like you.

(MOXIE *takes the glass and swallows the drink at a gulp*)

(*He takes the glass from her and puts it on the desk*) That's better. Now then. Chin up, keep a stiff upper lip, grit your teeth, put your shoulder to the wheel and—get cracking! (*He moves up* C *and offers her his arm*)

(MOXIE *puts on her spectacles, arranges her dress, laughs and moves to Crestwell*)

MOXIE (*taking his arm*) Oh, Fred.

CRESTWELL (*leading Moxie to the hall doors*) Have you read any good books lately?

They exit as—

the CURTAIN *falls*

SCENE 2

SCENE—*The same. An hour later. After dinner.*

When the CURTAIN *rises,* ALICE *is wandering about the room, humming to herself, collecting the used cocktail glasses and putting them on to her tray. She crosses to the desk and collects the empty glass. After a few moments* CRESTWELL *enters from the hall.*

CRESTWELL. Get a move on now, Alice. Mrs Crabbe will be wanting you in the kitchen.

ALICE. Yes, Mr Crestwell.

CRESTWELL (*crossing to* C) And might I suggest, Alice, in these few brief moments of intimacy that have been vouchsafed to us, that although understandably overwhelmed by the honour of being allowed to wait at table, there is no necessity to breathe quite so heavily while doing it.

ALICE. I'm sorry, Mr Crestwell.

CRESTWELL. When you approached the future Countess of Marshwood just now with the creamed carrots, you sounded like a goods train coming round a curve.

ALICE. I couldn't help it, really I couldn't. Seeing her tortured by the Japanese on Thursday and handing her carrots on Saturday, sort of took my breath away.

CRESTWELL. If it had really done that, Alice, there would be no cause for complaint.

ALICE. Yes, Mr Crestwell.

CRESTWELL. Nor was it entirely in accord with the higher traditions of domestic service, for you to stare at Mrs Moxton with your eyes bolting from your head and your mouth open.

ALICE. It was such a surprise, seeing her sitting at the table like that, dressed up to kill, I nearly had a fit.

CRESTWELL. If you are addicted to fits, Alice, you should have warned me in advance.

ALICE. What does it all mean, Mr Crestwell?

CRESTWELL. What does all what mean?

ALICE. About Mrs Moxton suddenly having meals with them instead of with us, and wearing her ladyship's bracelet?

CRESTWELL (*crossing to the table* R *of the sofa*) It is a social experiment based on the ancient and inaccurate assumption that, as we are equal in the eyes of God, we should therefore be equally equal in the eyes of our fellow creatures. (*He collects the cocktail glass from the table then moves above the sofa*)

ALICE. Oh!

CRESTWELL (*collecting the glass from the table above the sofa*) The fact that it doesn't work out like that and never will, in no way deters the idealists from pressing on valiantly towards Utopia. (*He crosses to* R *of Alice and puts the glasses on her tray*)

ALICE. What's Utopia?

CRESTWELL (*crossing to* L *of the sofa*) A spiritually hygienic abstraction, Alice, where everyone is hail-fellow-well-met and there is no waiting at table.

ALICE. Oh, I see, fork lunches.

(*The front door-bell rings off*)

CRESTWELL. The front door! Who the devil can that be? (*He*

crosses to the hall doors) Finish up now quickly, Alice, and go back to Mrs Crabbe.

ALICE. Yes, Mr Crestwell.

(CRESTWELL *exits hurriedly to the hall.* ALICE *puts the tray on the desk, picks up the ashtray from the desk, crosses and empties it into the ash-tray on the table above the sofa. Shen then replaces the empty ashtray on the desk, then empties the ashtray from the table above the sofa into the waste-paper basket. She picks up the tray of glasses and crosses to* C.

As she does so CRESTWELL *ushers* DON LUCAS *into the room.* ALICE, *with her mouth agape backs to* L *of the sofa and stands staring at Don, with her mouth open.* DON *is extremely handsome and in the late thirties. His skin is accurately tanned. His sports clothes are impeccable within the bounds of the best Hollywood tradition. He is also, very slightly, drunk. He moves and stands above the right end of the sofa)*

CRESTWELL *(standing in the open doorway)* I will inform his lordship that you are here.

DON *(turning to Crestwell)* Hey—wait a minute—don't do that. I don't know the earl, it isn't him I want to see. It's Miss Frayle I want to see, Miss Miranda Frayle.

CRESTWELL *(moving to* R *of Don)* Very good, sir.

DON. Before you tell her I'm here, could—*(he glances at Alice)* could I speak to you for a moment?

CRESTWELL *(crossing to* R *of Alice and leaning over her)* Take three deep breaths, Alice, through the nose. Keep the mouth rigidly closed, and hop it.

ALICE. Yes, Mr Crestwell.

(ALICE, *still staring at Don, crosses and exits to the hall)*

CRESTWELL *(moving below the left end of the sofa)* You were about to say, sir . . .

DON. Look here—I'm Don Lucas . . .

CRESTWELL. Yes, sir. I recognized you immediately. If I may say so, sir, with pleasure not unmixed with dismay.

DON. I don't get you.

CRESTWELL. I gather, sir, that you wish to speak to Miss Frayle—privately?

DON. Yeah—that's right—I do. Miss Frayle and me—well, we're very old friends.

CRESTWELL. It is the awareness of that fact, sir, that tinctured my spontaneous pleasure at seeing you with a modicum of apprehension.

DON. Come again?

CRESTWELL. Sequestered as we are, sir, in our remote Kentish vacuum, we are not entirely out of touch with the large world beyond. We have been privileged, thanks to the silver screen and the various periodicals appertaining to it, to follow both your public and private affairs with the keenest interest. You are a very popular figure in these parts, Mr Lucas.

Don. Thanks a lot. I could use a Scotch if you've got one handy.

Crestwell (*crossing to the table down* L) Certainly, sir. Would you like it in the form of a highball, straight, or on the rocks? (*He pours a whisky for Don*)

Don (*impressed*) Say! You're good. You know all the answers, don't you?

Crestwell (*turning*) Except the one to my question, sir.

Don. O.K. You win. On the rocks.

Crestwell. Very good, sir.

(Don *takes an American cigarette from his packet, and lights it.* Crestwell *crosses to Don and gives him the drink*)

Don. Thanks. (*He drinks*) What's your name?

Crestwell. Crestwell, sir. Frederick Crestwell.

Don. Now see here—(*he slaps Crestwell on the back*) Fred, I want your help. (*He leads Crestwell down* L *of the sofa*) I'm in a bit of a jam.

Crestwell. What kind of jam, sir? Professional, legal or emotional?

Don. With your fancy dialogue you could make a fortune in Hollywood as a script writer.

Crestwell. In my rare moments of melancholy introspection, sir, the idea has accurred to me, but I feel, on the whole, that I am happier where I am.

Don (*glancing towards the hall doors*) I want to talk to you as man to man.

Crestwell. Any other approach, sir, would be curious to say the least of it.

Don. This earl of yours. Is he really planning to marry Miranda—Miss Frayle, or is it just a publicity stunt? I want to know what's cooking.

Crestwell. If you're hungry, sir, after your long drive, I am sure I could rustle up a little cold chicken and a salad.

Don (*irritably*) O.K. Cut the comedy, Fred. This means a hell of a lot to me. I heard the news on the radio three days ago and hopped a plane right away. I've got to know whether it's the real McCoy, this marriage—(*he turns and crosses below the right end of the sofa*) or whether it's the studio publicity department pulling a fast one.

Crestwell. The real McCoy I'm afraid, sir.

Don. She can't do this to me. She just can't. (*He crosses to* R *of Crestwell*) I've got to see her, Fred, I've got to see her alone, now, and you've got to fix it.

Crestwell. They're all in the middle of dinner, sir. I don't see how I could extricate her, without "shooting the works", as you might say.

DON. You needn't say it's me. Say it's a reporter from *Life* magazine. She'd do anything for *Life* magazine.

CRESTWELL. An unaccountable impulse shared by so many public figures.

DON. Tell her it's a four page spread for the next issue with her picture on the cover. That'll fetch her. That'd fetch anybody.

CRESTWELL (*moving above the left end of the sofa*) I'll do my best, sir.

DON (*moving to* L *of Crestwell*) Fred, you're a pal. (*He takes a twenty-dollar bill from his pocket and hands it to Crestwell*) Here.

CRESTWELL (*looking at the bill*) Twenty dollars, sir! If the Government knew I had this I'd get a knighthood.

(CRESTWELL *crosses and exits to the hall, leaving the door open.* DON *crosses to the table down* L, *refills his glass, swallows the drink in one gulp then puts his glass on the table.*

After a few moments, MIRANDA *enters from the hall. As soon as she sees Don she hurriedly closes the door behind her and moves above the sofa*)

MIRANDA (*incredulously*) Pete!

DON (*turning; brokenly*) Pete!

MIRANDA (*furiously*) You son-of-a-bitch!

DON (*crossing to* L *of the sofa; brokenly*) Pete!

MIRANDA. Of all the low-down, mean tricks. I'll never forgive you for this. Never, never, never.

DON (*crossing to* L *of Miranda and attempting to embrace her*) Honey—I've got to talk to you—I've got to. I'm going out of my mind.

MIRANDA (*moving quickly down* R) Don't come near me. You—you snake!

DON (*moving above the right end of the sofa*) I've flown all across the Atlantic in a Stratoliner without even a sleeping berth on account of they were all full, and you call me a snake.

MIRANDA. You are, too, a snake. I never want to see you again. I told you that when I left, and it still goes.

DON. You don't mean that, Pete, not in your heart you don't.

MIRANDA. I do mean it. I've cut you out of my life, like—like a withered limb.

DON. Pete!

MIRANDA. And shut up calling me Pete. That's all over.

DON (*moving to* L *of her; with a slight show of spirit*) I'm no withered limb and you know it. (*He grips her by the shoulders*) Look at me.

MIRANDA (*struggling*) Let me alone.

DON (*violently kissing her*) Now then, am I a withered limb?

MIRANDA (*freeing herself*) How could you—oh, how could you!

DON. I'm crazy about you. I've been crazy about you for three whole years.

MIRANDA (*contemptuously*) Crazy about me! What about Beejie

Lemaire, and Zenda Hicks and that phoney Polish princess that Daryl Zanuck gave the party for?

Don. They didn't mean a thing to me, not a thing, you know they didn't. They were just ships that pass in the night.

Miranda. Maybe they were, but they certainly passed through your beach house in Santa Monica on their way to the open sea.

Don (*crossing to* LC) So we're back at that again, are we?

Miranda. You bet your life we're back at that. I gave you all I had to give; my heart, my dreams, my tenderness . . . (*She turns her back to him*)

Don. Everything but equal billing. Remember *Be Still Foolish Heart?*

Miranda (*turning and moving below the sofa*) You were featured under the title, which considering it was your first big picture was more than you had a right to expect.

Don. I got the notices anyway.

Miranda. You got a rave in the *Hollywood Reporter*, and your pants torn off you in the *New Yorker*. If you call that "getting the notices", I'll take vanilla. (*She crosses to* R *of him*)

Don (*incensed*) We needn't worry about that any more though, need we? I'm bigger box office now than you ever were, even before you started slipping.

Miranda (*outraged*) Started slipping!

Don. Do you think I don't know why you're marrying this titled guy? Do you think the whole world doesn't know? It's because you're on the skids and have been ever since *Catherine the Great*.

Miranda (*angrily*) On the skids, am I? It may interest you to know that M.G.M. have offered me anything I like to ask to do *The Wicked Years*. They've been badgering me for weeks.

Don. They've been badgering every star in Hollywood to do that lousy script for the last eighteen months.

Miranda. Get out, Don! I'm sick of this. Get out!

Don. I'm not getting out of anywhere until I'm good and ready. There are a few things I'd like to say to this earl of yours.

(Miranda *gives a quick frightened look towards the hall doors, then crosses to* R *of Don and changes her tactics*)

Miranda. Don, please go—please. For the sake of all we've meant to each other, for the sake of all the good times we've had don't come busting in here and making a scene and spoiling everything. Please!

Don. Do you love this guy?

Miranda. Yes, of course I do.

Don. Really love him? (*He draws Miranda tenderly to him*) As much as you loved me?

Miranda (*in acute distress*) Please, please go, Don—they'll be here in a minute.

DON (*inexorably*) As much as you loved me?

MIRANDA. It's different. I mean no people love other people in the same way.

DON. I'm crazy about you, Pete. (*He places her head on his right shoulder*) I've fought against it. I've tried to forget you. Ever since we had the row, ever since the night when we said good-bye and you threw the Film Academy Award for nineteen-forty-nine at me, I've tried to get you out of my mind, out of my heart . . .

(MIRANDA *lifts her head from his shoulder and stops him speaking by touching his mouth*)

MIRANDA (*moved*) Don't—please don't say any more.

DON. Pete!

MIRANDA. Go away, you've got to go away.

DON (*gallantly*) O.K., I'll go. (*He moves up* LC *and gazes sadly out of the french windows*) I know we're all washed up. I know now that there isn't any more hope for me. I only just wanted to make sure. (*He turns and looks wistfully at her*)

(MIRANDA *moves to* R *of Don and touches his arm*)

Good-bye, Pete. It was swell while it lasted.

MIRANDA (*tremulously*) Good-bye, Pete.

(DON *very gently and tenderly takes Miranda in his arms and kisses her.*

FELICITY *enters from the hall.* MIRANDA *and* DON *spring apart.* DON *moves down* L *of Miranda*)

FELICITY (*standing in the open doorway*) I really came to rescue you, Miranda, but I see that it was unnecessary. (*She moves down* R *of the sofa*)

MIRANDA (*pointing to Don; with commendable presence of mind*) This is one of my very old friends. We were just saying good-bye.

FELICITY. But surely he has only just arrived?

DON. I've got to get back to London.

MIRANDA (*pointing at Don; with poise*) This is Don Lucas. (*She points to Felicity*) Don, this is Lady Marshwood.

FELICITY (*enthusiastically*) I thought I recognized you but I simply couldn't believe my eyes.

(DON *crosses below the sofa to Felicity and shakes hands with her*)

This is the most delightful surprise.

DON (*gratified*) Thank you, ma'am.

FELICITY. You're surely not intending to drive all the way to London now?

DON. I'm afraid I must—I . . .

FELICITY. Nonsense! I won't hear of it. That long dreary road at this time of night, in the pouring rain.

MIRANDA. It isn't raining.

FELICITY. It will be by the time he gets to Canterbury. I've never known it fail. Besides I couldn't dream of allowing Mr Don Lucas to creep into the house and out again without letting anybody know. I should be stoned by the entire village.

MIRANDA (*crossing to* L *of Don*) He's got to get to London to-night. He has an important conference the first thing in the morning.

DON. I have?

FELICITY. Who ever heard of people having conferences on Sunday mornings. (*She crosses to the fireplace and rings the bell*) Mr Lucas, I absolutely insist on you staying until tomorrow at least.

MIRANDA (*crossing below Don to* R *of him*) But—Lady Marshwood—really . . .

FELICITY (*moving down* R; *gaily*) Dear Miranda. You really must allow me to have my own way. You're not married to Nigel yet, you know; I am still mistress of this house, and I intend to rule you all with a rod of iron until the last possible moment. (*To Don*) Crestwell can supply you with anything you need in the way of pyjamas and razors and toothbrushes. Please, Mr Lucas. I shall be terribly hurt if you refuse.

MIRANDA. But . . .

DON (*with a glance at Miranda*) Thanks a lot, Lady Marshwood. (*He sits on the sofa at the left end*) I'd like to.

MIRANDA. Don! (*She stares at him and crosses down* LC)

(CRESTWELL *enters from the hall*)

CRESTWELL. You rang, Milady? (*He moves to* R *of the sofa*)

(MIRANDA *moves to the downstage pillar of the alcove and leans against it*)

FELICITY. Oh, Crestwell. Mr Don Lucas will be staying the night. You will see that he has everything he wants, won't you?

CRESTWELL. Certainly, Milady. The Japanese room?

FELICITY. Yes. (*She crosses to* R *of Don*) You haven't got any feeling about being in a Japanese room, have you? I mean you weren't in the Pacific or anything?

DON (*rising*) No, ma'am.

FELICITY. I'm so glad. It isn't all that Japanese anyhow—(*she sits on the sofa at the right end*) just the wallpaper and rather a washy looking painting of some carp.

(DON *sits* L *of Felicity on the sofa.* CRESTWELL *moves down* R)

It has a lovely view and when it's really clear you can see Dover Castle. Have you ever been to Dover Castle?

DON. No, ma'am. I've never been to England before.

FELICITY. I'm afraid that what with the Festival and one thing and another you haven't chosen the best time to come, but we still have quite a lot to be proud of. (*To Crestwell*) Tell his lordship that Mr Lucas has arrived, will you, Crestwell, and ask them all to hurry up. We'll have coffee in here.

CRESTWELL. Very good, Milady.

(CRESTWELL *exits to the hall, closing the doors behind him*)

FELICITY. How extraordinary to think that the last time I saw you and dear Miranda together you were carrying her, practically naked, through a burning village. Would you like a drink?

DON (*rising*) Thanks—thanks a lot. (*He crosses a little unsteadily to the table down* L *and refills his glass*)

(MIRANDA, *as* DON *passes her, glares at him*)

FELICITY. It's all over there, do help yourself. (*To Miranda*) You don't want to go back into the dining-room, do you, Miranda and have any more of that disgusting sweet?

(DON *picks up his glass and moves into the alcove*)

MIRANDA (*resignedly*) No, thank you.

FELICITY. Then sit down, dear, and relax.

(MIRANDA *sits in the chair down* L)

I think we should all relax really. It's been a tremendously exciting day, what with you and Nigel arriving and Mr Lucas suddenly appearing out of the night, and the garden overrun with Girl Guides . . .

DON. Girl Guides?

FELICITY. It's a very English institution. I don't know if you have them in Hollywood. It's a splendid idea, really. They're trained to do practically everything from artificial respiration to making fires with damp twigs. (*She rises and crosses below the sofa to Don*) If the news leaks out that you're here, Mr Lucas, they'll probably attack the house in mass formation.

(NIGEL *enters from the hall, leaving the door open. His expression is a trifle forbidding. He crosses to* R *of the desk*)

(*To Nigel. Cheerfully*) Ah, there you are, Nigel. This is Mr Don Lucas—my son, Lord Marshwood.

DON (*crossing below Felicity to* L *of Nigel*) Hello, there. (*He shakes hands with Nigel*)

NIGEL (*unenthusiastically*) How do you do?

FELICITY. He's driven all the way from London to say good-bye to Miranda. They're old friends, you know.

NIGEL (*with a look at Miranda*) Yes, I do know.

FELICITY. And believe it or not he intended to drive all the way back again immediately. Have you ever heard of anything so absurd? Fortunately I was able to persuade him to stay the night at least.

NIGEL. Stay the night!

Felicity. Yes. Don't worry. Crestwell has everything under control. We've decided on the Japanese room because of the view.

Nigel. Of course. A very good idea. (*He crosses below the sofa to the fireplace*) How thoughtful of you, Mother.

(Miranda *rises, glares at Don, then crosses to Nigel.*

Lady Hayling, *the* Admiral, Moxie *and* Peter *enter from the hall.* Felicity *moves up* c. Lady Hayling *moves to* r *of Felicity. The* Admiral *moves to* r *of Lady Hayling.* Moxie *moves down* r. Peter *stands above the right end of the sofa*)

Felicity (*leading* Lady Hayling *to Don*) Cynthia—this is Mr Don Lucas. He obviously doesn't need any introduction, really, does he? (*To Don*) Lady Hayling.

Lady Hayling (*crossing below Felicity and shaking hands with Don*) How do you do?

(Felicity *moves below the left end of the sofa.* Miranda *sits in the chair* r)

Felicity (*introducing*) Mrs Moxton—Mr Lucas—Admiral Hayling, and my nephew Peter.

(Moxie, Don, *the* Admiral *and* Peter *murmur "How do you do?"*)

(*Conversationally*) This is the first time Mr Lucas has ever been to England. Imagine!

(Crestwell *enters from the hall. He carries a tray with coffee*)

Lady Hayling. How extraordinary. (*To Don*) I do hope you're enjoying it.

Don. Yes, ma'am.

(Felicity *moves the table* l *of the sofa and places it below the sofa, then sits on the sofa at the left end.* Lady Hayling *crosses and sits in the chair down* l)

Admiral (*crossing to* r *of Don*) I was in America once in nineteen twenty-two. Norfolk, Virginia. Do you know it?

(Crestwell *crosses above the sofa to* l *of it and puts the tray on the table below the sofa.* Moxie *moves to* Peter *and they stand above the sofa.* Peter *offers Moxie a cigarette and lights it for her.* Moxie *puts her bag on the table above the sofa*)

Don. No, sir.

Admiral. I was commanding a light cruiser squadron in the West Indies. We had to put in at Norfolk because of boiler trouble. It was damned hot.

(Crestwell *arranges the coffee cups*)

FELICITY. Boiler trouble sounds hot, anyhow, doesn't it? Thank you, Crestwell. You might put up the bridge table in the study, I think. We may want to play later.

CRESTWELL. Very good, Milady.

(CRESTWELL *crosses and exits down* R)

FELICITY (*pouring the coffee*) Do you play bridge, Mr Lucas?

DON. No, ma'am. I guess poker's more in my line.

FELICITY. My late husband adored poker. What a pity he isn't here.

PETER (*to Don*) Are you going to be in England long?

DON. No. I've got to get back. I've got to start on a new picture.

FELICITY. How exciting. What is it to be about, or is that a secret?

DON (*looking fixedly at Miranda*) No, it's no secret. (*He moves and stands above the left end of the sofa*) It's an old story, the oldest story in the world, it's about a bum.

FELICITY. What an odd subject for a moving picture.

PETER. Felicity, bum doesn't mean quite the same in America as it does in England.

DON (*staring at Miranda; unsteadily*) A bum is a guy who hasn't any place to go, who hasn't got anything to live for, who just bums around wishing he was dead.

MIRANDA (*in an effort to quell him*) Don!

FELICITY (*to Don*) It sounds very sad. Will it have a happy ending?

DON (*brokenly*) No, ma'am—that's not the way it goes—that's not the way it goes at all—excuse me.

(DON *turns and exits hurriedly by the french windows, taking his drink with him*)

FELICITY (*after a slight pause*) Poor Mr Lucas. (*She puts down the coffee-pot*) He seems upset about something. You'd better go after him, Peter, and for Heaven's sake keep him away from the shrubbery—if Elsie Mumby sees him she'll give a wolf call.

PETER. All right.

(PETER *crosses and exits hurriedly by the french windows. The* ADMIRAL *moves to the coffee table, takes two cups of coffee, crosses to Lady Hayling, and hands one to her.* MOXIE *moves below the sofa*)

NIGEL. Did you know he was coming, Miranda?

(FELICITY *hands* MOXIE *two cups of coffee. She passes one to Miranda*)

MIRANDA. Of course I didn't.

(MOXIE *sits on the sofa at the right end*)

Nigel (*crossing to the coffee table*) I think it was very inconsiderate of you to ask him to stay, Mother. (*He picks up a cup of coffee and crosses to* L *of the sofa*)

Felicity. It would have been far more inconsiderate to have let him go all the way back to London in the middle of the night. Not only inconsiderate but thoroughly inhospitable.

Nigel. I was thinking of Miranda.

Felicity. He is, too. That's what's upsetting him. We really must do all we possibly can to cheer him up.

(Nigel *moves to* R *of the desk*)

I rather wish now that we'd given him the old nursery instead of the Japanese room. It has a lovely frieze of rabbits that you liked so much when you were little. (*She sips her coffee*)

(Crestwell *enters down* R *and crosses to* R *of the sofa*)

Crestwell. The bridge table is ready, Milady.

Felicity. Thank you, Crestwell. You'd better leave the coffee things, we may need some more.

Crestwell. Very good, Milady.

(Crestwell *exits to the hall, closing the doors behind him.* Nigel, *obviously suspecting some sort of plot, is very angry. He moves below the sofa and puts his cup on the coffee table*)

Nigel (*icily*) You asked me before dinner, Mother, when Miranda and I were going to be married.

Felicity. Of course I did, darling. We're all dying to know.

Nigel. And I replied, if you remember, "As soon as possible".

Felicity. Certainly I remember.

Nigel. Well, I've changed my mind.

Miranda (*rising*) Nigel!

(Felicity *looks at Moxie*)

Nigel. It's going to be sooner than possible. It's going to be on Monday. I have the licence already. We shall drive up to London in the morning and be married in the afternoon.

Felicity. Isn't that a little impulsive, dear?

(Miranda *puts her cup on the table* R *of the sofa*)

Nigel. I don't care how impulsive it is. That's how it's going to be.

Moxie (*rising*) That's not how it's going to be. (*She crosses down* R *and puts her cup on the table down* R)

Felicity. Moxie—please . . .

Nigel (*to Moxie*) I fail to see that this is any business of yours.

Moxie (*in great distress*) I'm sorry, Milady—I can't bear it any more, really I can't.

Nigel. What are you talking about?

MOXIE. About you and Miss Miranda Frayle, My Lord. You're not going to marry her on Monday, nor any other day of the week. You're not going to marry her at all.

NIGEL } *(together)* What's the matter with you? Have you gone out of your mind?

FELICITY } *(together)* Nigel, please. (*She rises and crosses to* L *of Moxie*) Moxie, dear, for Heaven's sake don't say any more. It won't do any good.

(MIRANDA *crosses and sits on the sofa at the left end*)

MOXIE. I'm sorry if you think I'm letting you down, Milady, but I can't go through with it any longer, it doesn't feel right and it isn't right and I shouldn't ever have started it in the first place.

(FELICITY *crosses to* R *of Moxie*)

(*To Nigel*) As he's gone this far, I would like his lordship to know a few of the facts before he marries my sister. (*She removes her spectacles and crosses to* R *of Miranda*)

MIRANDA. My God! Dora!

MOXIE. That's right, dear, Dora! The one who ill-treated you when she was drunk and died in sordid circumstances.

FELICITY. Oh dear! This has really got out of control.

MIRANDA. What are you doing here? I don't understand—I thought you were dead.

MOXIE. You never thought any such thing, you never cared whether I was dead or alive. Well, more fool you, because here I am alive and kicking, and if you think you're going to flounce about as mistress of this house which has been my home for nineteen years, you've got another think coming.

NIGEL (*moving above the sofa and standing up* R) Take her upstairs, Mother, for God's sake.

MIRANDA (*rising; with grandeur*) Please, Nigel. I'd like to go to my room if you don't mind. This is all too unpleasant. (*She moves* L *of the sofa to Nigel*)

(MOXIE *moves* R *of the sofa and stubs out her cigarette in the ashtray on the table* R *of the sofa*)

MOXIE (*moving between Miranda and the hall door*) Just a minute. You're going to listen to what I have to say if it's the last thing you do, and it's no use playing the fine madame any more either, because the cat's out of the bag and all the airs and graces in the world won't put it back again.

MIRANDA (*furiously*) This is insufferable! (*She turns and starts to move* L)

MOXIE (*holding Miranda and turning her*) You're dead right it's insufferable. It all sounds very touching, you standing in the slum gazing up at the window of the room where your mother died, but it may interest you to know that your mum died in St Thomas's Hospital. And ten to one she wouldn't have died at all if you hadn't broken her heart by behaving like a tart and running off to America with that greasy little agent.

Miranda. How dare you speak to me like that! (*She moves to* L *of the chair* R, *turns and faces Moxie*) Don't listen to her, Nigel. Don't listen to her.

Moxie. It's all true, Freda, and you know it. And I wouldn't have said a word about it if you hadn't started showing off and making out that you were brought up in the gutter. Poverty and squalor indeed! A London Cockney born within the sound of Bow Bells. You were born at number three Station Road, Sidcup, and if you can hear the sound of Bow Bells from Sidcup, you must have the ears of an elk-hound.

Miranda (*putting her hands to her head*) I can't bear any more. I can't—I can't. Take me away, Nigel—take me away. (*She throws herself on to the sofa*)

Moxie. If his lordship takes you away and marries you three times over, it won't alter the fact that I'm your sister. You'd better remember that.

Felicity. I really think, Moxie, that you've said enough.

Moxie (*moving to* L *of Felicity*) Not quite, Milady, there's still a bit more and my heart's heavy with it. I've got to leave this house for good, first thing in the morning. I can't be your ladyship's maid any longer, not with the best will in the world I can't. It's all over and done with. (*Brokenly*) Good-bye, Milady.

Moxie *sobs, turns and runs into the hall as—*

the Curtain *falls*

ACT III

SCENE—*The same. The following morning.*

When the CURTAIN *rises it is about nine-thirty. Church bells are heard in the distance.* PETER *is lying on the sofa leaning against the left end. He is smoking a cigarette and reading "The Observer".* CRESTWELL *enters from the hall.*

CRESTWELL. You rang, sir?

PETER. Yes, Crestwell. I'm feeling lonely. The house is like a tomb. Where is everybody?

CRESTWELL (*moving to* R *of the sofa*) His lordship went out very early, sir. He said he was going for a long ride. Her ladyship was called at the usual time, but she hasn't come down yet. Miss Frayle hasn't rung for her breakfast, neither has Mr Lucas.

PETER. What about Moxie?

CRESTWELL. Very low spirited, sir. She's packing.

PETER. She's really going?

CRESTWELL. Yes, to Bexhill, sir. She says she has friends tnere. She's catching the eleven-fifteen from Deal. It means three changes, but she's adamant.

PETER. Oh Lord! Poor Moxie. It does seem damned unfair.

CRESTWELL. I feel that it would be premature to abandon too hastily all hope of a happy ending, sir. Mrs Moxton, in common with most of her sex, is inclined to allow her emotions to run away with her. Her ladyship, on the other hand, is not.

PETER. I hope you're right, Crestwell.

CRESTWELL. If you'll forgive an archaic Shavianism, sir, I'm bloody sure I'm right.

(DON *enters from the hall. The sound of the bells fades*)

PETER. Hello! How are you?

DON (*crossing slowly above the sofa to* L *of it*) Terrible.

PETER. Hangover?

DON. You know, pal, you could make a packet telling people's fortunes.

CRESTWELL. A Horse's Neck will soon put you right, sir.

DON. It'd take a Giraffe's Neck to make me even able to walk, let alone drive a car.

(PETER *swings his legs off the sofa and stubs out his cigarette in the ashtray on the table* L *of the sofa*)

CRESTWELL. You're not thinking of leaving, sir?

Don. You bet I am. I'm getting the hell out of here as soon as I can see out of my eyes.

Crestwell. Leave it to me, sir, we'll have you ticking over in no time. Excuse me.

(Crestwell *exits hurriedly to the hall*)

Peter. Why don't you sit down?

Don. Because if I did, I'd stay down.

Peter. Last night in the garden you promised me that you'd pull yourself together and face the future with a smile.

Don. That was last night. This is today.

Peter. You haven't been crying again, have you?

Don. Listen, Pete. . . . (*He breaks off*) Oh God! (*He puts his hand to his head and turns towards the french windows*)

Peter. What's the matter?

Don (*turning*) Calling you Pete. It kind of slipped out.

Peter. I don't mind a bit.

Don (*crossing to the french windows*) There's only one Pete in the world for me. (*He gazes out of the window*)

Peter. I'm sure it's very charming of you to say so.

Don (*turning and moving to the alcove step*) You were wonderful to me last night, just wonderful, and if you think I'll ever forget it you're plumb crazy. We're friends, aren't we?

Peter. Of course we are.

Don. It's great to hear you say that, it is honestly.

Peter. I'm so glad.

Don. Friendship's a rare thing, one of the rarest things in the whole God-damned world. (*He moves down* LC) Do you mind shaking hands on it?

Peter (*rising and moving to* R *of Don*) Not in the least, if you feel it's really necessary.

Don (*gripping Peter firmly by the hand*) Attaboy!

(Felicity *enters from the hall, closing the doors*)

Felicity. What on earth are you doing?

Peter (*over his shoulder*) Shaking hands.

Felicity (*moving down* R) Good morning, Mr Lucas. You're just the one I wanted to see. Peter, be a darling and go into the garden for a minute, will you?

Peter. I'm getting rather sick of the garden.

Felicity (*indicating the door down* R) The study then, anywhere.

(Peter *crosses to the door down* R, *taking the newspaper with him*)

I want to talk to Mr Lucas privately.

Peter. O.K., pal.

(Peter *exits down* R)

Felicity. Do sit down, Mr Lucas—Don. (*She sits on the sofa at the right end and pats the seat beside her*)

(Don *sits* L *of Felicity on the sofa*)

You don't mind if I call you Don, do you? I feel somehow as if we were old friends.

Don. Thank you, ma'am.

Felicity. And you must call me Felicity.

(Crestwell *enters from the hall. He carries a tray with a glass of brandy and ginger-ale and some aspirin. He crosses above the sofa to* L *of it*)

Ma'am sounds so royal. It makes me feel as though I were opening something.

Crestwell. Your Horse's Neck, sir.

Don. Thanks. (*He takes the drink*)

Crestwell. Swallow the three aspirin first, sir, and then sip the drink slowly.

(Don *takes the aspirin*)

Felicity (*brightly*) Quite like old times, isn't it, Crestwell? Except that the late Lord Marshwood always chewed the aspirin.

(Don *drinks*)

Crestwell. Young Willis is here, Milady. He's been here since eight-fifteen.

Felicity. Tell him to wait, Crestwell. We might have a splendid scoop for him later.

Crestwell. Very good, Milady.

(Crestwell *crosses and exits to the hall, closing the door behind him*)

Don. I guess I got a bit high last night and acted like a heel. I'm sorry.

Felicity. Even if you had acted like the highest heel, Don, I should have understood. After all, you were under considerable emotional stress, weren't you?

Don. Yeah. I guess I was.

Felicity. And you still are?

Don (*vehemently*) Ma'am—Felicity. I'm going to snap out of it. I know when I'm licked.

Felicity. Courage, Don, courage.

Don. I shouldn't have come busting down here and shooting off my mouth and making a fool of myself. I see that now. It's no good being crazy about somebody if they're not crazy about you, is it? We were all washed up, Miranda and me, a long while ago, only I was too dumb to believe it.

Felicity. Are you so sure?

Don. How do you mean?

Felicity. I am Nigel's mother and therefore what I am going to say is doubly difficult. Can I trust you? Really trust you?

Don. Sure you can.

Felicity. I'm also a sentimentalist, and I've always believed, foolishly perhaps, that when two people really love each other, nothing in the world should be allowed to break it. This proposed marriage between Miranda and my son is a mistake, a tragic, ghastly mistake, because you are the one she loves, the only one she will ever truly love. She told me so.

Don (*incredulously*) Told you so?

Felicity (*with a gentle smile*) Not in so many words, but I am a woman, Don, and I knew at once when I saw you together, from the expression in her eyes when she looked at you, the tone of her voice when she spoke to you, that her heart, her obstinate, capricious heart, belonged to you.

Don. She told me I was a snake and she never wanted to see me again. She said I was a withered limb.

Felicity. People never say things like that unless they're passionately in love. I'm surprised at you, Don, I am really.

Don (*putting his glass on the table* L *of the sofa and rising*) What the hell can I do? (*He moves down* LC) She's going to be married. It's all set.

Felicity. I'm disappointed in you, Don. When I think of your presence of mind and resource in that burning village, and look at you now . . .

Don. That was a movie. (*He crosses below the sofa and faces down* R) Real life doesn't work out like movies.

Felicity. Not as a general rule, I admit, but I see no reason why it shouldn't just every now and then.

Don (*turning*) But what can I do?

Felicity (*rising*) Don't do anything. Just wait. Above all keep up your courage and don't admit defeat.

(Nigel *enters by the french windows. He wears riding clothes*)

(*She turns*) Good morning, darling. Did you enjoy your ride?

Nigel. No.

Felicity (*turning towards the door down* R *and calling*) Peter.

Nigel (*moving down* L; *sullenly to Don*) Good morning. I hope you slept all right.

Don (*embarrassed*) Oh yes—thanks.

(Peter *enters down* R *and crosses below Don to* R *of Felicity*)

Peter (*as he enters*) What's happening?

Felicity. You ought to know better than to ask that, dear—nothing whatever happens on Sunday mornings. Don wants to see the church, don't you, Don? I thought you might like to show it to him. (*To Don*) The tower's Norman but the rest of it's a good deal later.

DON. Later.

FELICITY. You might show him old Mrs Dunlop's cottage while you're at it. It isn't far.

PETER. I don't mind the church but I draw the line at old Mrs Dunlop.

FELICITY. Oh she's much better. (*She crosses to* L *of Don*) She's been happy as a sandboy since her husband died. (*She pats Don's back*) Run along, both of you.

DON (*crossing to* L *of the sofa*) O.K., ma'am—Felicity.

PETER (*resignedly*) Come on then.

(DON *and* PETER *cross and exit by the french windows.* NIGEL *moves down* LC)

FELICITY. Ma'am Felicity sounds so domestically American, doesn't it? Like Grandma Moses or Mother Goddam. (*She moves* L *of the sofa to the desk*)

NIGEL (*crossing and standing down* R *of the sofa*) I want to talk to you, Mother.

FELICITY (*drawing the desk chair to the desk and sitting*) Not just now, darling. I've got a million things to do before church. Mrs Crabbe is waiting for the menus and young Willis has been here since eight-fifteen.

NIGEL. Young Willis?

FELICITY. Yes, dear. If neither you nor Miranda will give him an interview, I shall have to. I do think that our first allegiance should be to the *Kentish Times*. You needn't be afraid I shall be indiscreet. I shall just fob him off with some of those stories about Miranda's early life. The fact they're not strictly accurate won't matter in the least. They'll give him something to go on. (*She picks up a paper and writes a menu on a sheet of paper*)

NIGEL. You're not to say a word to young Willis about Miranda's early life. I absolutely forbid it.

FELICITY. It can't possibly affect you, darling. The interview won't be out until the middle of the week, and you and Miranda will be away on your honeymoon. I presume you're going to have a honeymoon somewhere, aren't you?

NIGEL. It's no use trying to deceive me, Mother. It's no use trying to pretend after last night that everything's all right, because you know damn well it isn't.

FELICITY. What happened last night was embarrassing I admit, but I can't see that it alters the situation in any way.

NIGEL. Mother!

FELICITY. You said, rather loudly I thought, that you had a special licence and were going to marry Miranda tomorrow afternoon. Well, that's that, isn't it? I think it's rather hard on the village people, of course. (*She picks up her spectacles from the desk and puts them on*) Everybody was so thrilled. After all, we haven't had any real excitement here since that ship foundered off the South Foreland.

NIGEL (*moving down* R) I'm distracted, Mother. I haven't slept a wink all night. Have you seen Miranda this morning?

FELICITY. No. Have you? (*She resumes working on the menu*)

NIGEL. No.

FELICITY. Then I think you should. She's probably fairly distracted, too.

NIGEL (*crossing below the sofa to Felicity*) You don't like her, do you?

FELICITY. Of course I don't. I think she's a perfect ass.

NIGEL. Mother!

FELICITY (*turning to him*) Well, what could be more asinine than inventing all that nonsense about slums and pubs and gutters, when all the time she was born perfectly respectably at Sidcup? (*She resumes work*)

NIGEL. She was romanticizing herself. I don't see any particular harm in that. After all her whole life has been spent romanticizing herself, and very successfully, too. I expect it's become a habit.

FELICITY. Well, she'll have to break herself of it. We can't have the new Lady Marshwood wandering about the countryside telling the most appalling lies to everybody.

NIGEL. She was naturally a bit nervous and ill at ease, she probably wasn't thinking what she was saying. (*He crosses down* R)

FELICITY. She seemed quite at ease to me, sitting there sipping away at that disgusting lemonade. Why couldn't she have a nice healthy Martini like everyone else?

NIGEL. That's unreasonable and unkind.

FELICITY. You remind me so much of your father at moments.

NIGEL. What's that got to do with it?

FELICITY. He'd never look twice at a woman unless she had an ineradicable streak of commonness. I could always trust him at house-parties but never at race meetings.

NIGEL. He loved you, didn't he?

FELICITY. Good Heavens, no. (*She removes her glasses and turns in her chair to face Nigel*) Not in that way. He developed a sort of rugged affection for me but he was never remotely attracted to me. He told me on our honeymoon that I had Sloane Street feet.

(*She puts on her spectacles, turns and resumes work*)

NIGEL. Well, perhaps he'd have been able to think of a way out of this situation. I'm damned if I can.

FELICITY. Neither can I. Isn't it maddening?

NIGEL. Of all the incredible horrible coincidences.

FELICITY. I quite agree. But there it is, and we shall just have to rise above it, shan't we?

NIGEL (*moving up* R) Is Moxie going?

FELICITY. Yes. To Bexhill. She's catching the eleven-fifteen from Deal.

NIGEL. Bexhill?

FELICITY. It's quite a charming place I believe. I shall join her there in a few days when all the fuss is over. She doesn't know that, of course, because she's in too much of a state at the moment to see anything very clearly, poor darling.

NIGEL. You can't go and live at Bexhill.

FELICITY. I didn't say I was going to live there. I shall just stay in an hotel for a few days, while I decide where I'm going to lay my old bones permanently.

NIGEL. Old bones indeed! (*He moves below the sofa*) You haven't the slightest intention of leaving this house and you never had.

FELICITY (*removing her spectacles and putting them on the desk*) There you're wrong. When you marry Miranda I shall certainly leave this house. Watching her doing that embroidery would give me a nervous collapse in a week.

NIGEL (*crossing to* LC) How can I marry her now? In these circumstances?

FELICITY. You can't not marry somebody just because they didn't dance to a barrel organ when they were five.

NIGEL. I think your flippancy is unforgivable, Mother, and in the worst possible taste.

FELICITY (*rising and replacing the desk chair*) It's no use abusing me, darling. You've made your bed and publicly announced your intention of lying on it as soon as possible. (*She moves down* C) I don't see how you can get out of it now. It's too late.

NIGEL (*moving up* C) I didn't say I wanted to get out of it. I merely said, "How can I marry Miranda in these circumstances?" And I say it again. How can I?

FELICITY (*moving above the left end of the sofa*) How does Miranda feel about it?

NIGEL (*moving down* R) I don't know. She went to bed in floods of tears last night and slammed the door.

FELICITY (*moving below the sofa to* L *of Nigel*) Well, if I were you, dear, I should take her for a nice long walk and just hammer away until you arrive at a solution, or better still, take the car and a picnic lunch and go to St Margaret's Bay.

(DON *and* PETER *enter by the french windows. They are both breathing heavily.* DON *is dabbing his hand with his handkerchief*)

(*She turns*) Good Heavens! Back so soon?

PETER (*crossing to* L *of the sofa*) We couldn't get through the gates. The whole village is out.

(DON *crosses to* R *of Peter*)

FELICITY. Why, Don—what have you done to your hand?

Peter. It's red ink from Elsie Mumby's pen.

Felicity. Show him where to wash, Peter.

Peter (*crossing above Don to the hall door*) This way—if it dries it will never come off.

(Don *crosses to* Peter, *and they exit to the hall*)

Felicity. I had a feeling when I woke up this morning that today was going to be difficult and I was quite right.

Nigel (*pointing to the hall door*) Is that lachrymose oaf going to stay with us indefinitely?

Felicity. He's not an oaf, he's perfectly charming and if you had any sense of *noblesse oblige* you'd ask him to be your best man. (*She crosses to the desk and picks up the menu*)

Nigel (*bitterly*) Thank you for everything, Mother. You've been a great comfort to me.

(Nigel *moves up* R *and exits to the hall, leaving the door open.* Felicity *studies her menu.*

After a few moments Crestwell *enters from the hall. He carries a tray with a large pile of autograph books on it*)

Crestwell (*moving down* R) Shall I put this lot with the others, Milady?

Felicity. Yes please, Crestwell. And you'd better tell young Willis to go away. I fear we shall have no definite news until later in the day.

Crestwell. Yes, Milady.

Felicity (*moving above the sofa*) And, Crestwell, you might have Mr Lucas's car brought round. We may be needing it. Did you give Miss Frayle my message?

Crestwell. Yes, Milady. She should be down soon.

Felicity. How did she look?

Crestwell. A bit papery, Milady. I don't think she slept very well. She enquired about trains to London. I told her there was an eleven-fifteen from Deal but that she'd have to change at Ashford and Maidstone.

Felicity. I can't think why that train ever leaves at all. (*She moves down* LC) It doesn't seem to go anywhere that anybody wants.

(Miranda *enters from the hall. She is looking pale and wears black. She carries a raincoat and a handbag. She throws the raincoat on to the chair up* R, *then crosses to the table above the sofa and puts her handbag on it*)

Crestwell. Will that be all for the moment, Milady?

Felicity (*moving to the desk*) Yes, thank you, Crestwell.

(Crestwell *exits down* R, *taking the autograph books with him*)

Good morning, Miranda. I do hope you slept well.

Miranda (*moving below the sofa*) I hardly slept at all.

FELICITY (*moving down* LC) You poor dear, you must be exhausted. Would you like some coffee or Bovril or anything?

MIRANDA. No, thank you. Your butler said that you wanted to speak to me urgently.

FELICITY. How idiotic of him. It isn't in the least urgent. I only wanted to ask you a favour.

MIRANDA. A favour?

FELICITY. Yes. I want you to grant an exclusive interview to our local paper. I know you're badgered to death by such things as a rule, but Willis is one of my special protégés and it would mean so much to him.

MIRANDA. I'm afraid I can't, Lady Marshwood. I'm going away.

FELICITY. Going away?

MIRANDA. I don't feel that I could possibly stay, not as long as my sister's in the house.

FELICITY. But she lives here. She's lived here for nineteen years.

MIRANDA. I don't care where she lives. I never want to set eyes on her again.

FELICITY. I'm afraid that's impossible. I couldn't move without her. I'm devoted to her.

MIRANDA (*moving down* R *and standing with her back to Felicity*) She insulted me and humiliated me, and I shall never speak to her until the end of my days.

FELICITY. I don't suppose she'll mind that. After all, you haven't been exactly intimate for the last twenty years, have you?

MIRANDA. The situation is impossible.

FELICITY. Difficult, I grant you, but not impossible. Moxie and I won't be in the house all the time, you know. We shall go away sometimes—on little visits.

MIRANDA (*turning; horrified*) Do you mean that you are going on living here after we're married?

FELICITY. Naturally, my dear. It happens to be my home, you know. I lived here steadily through Nigel's first marriage. Of course it didn't last very long, but that wasn't my fault. At least, I don't think it was.

MIRANDA. And Dora—Moxie—whatever you call her—she'll live here, too?

FELICITY. Of course.

MIRANDA. But it's quite out of the question. It would be intolerable.

FELICITY. It would be much more intolerable for me if she went away.

MIRANDA. But you must see . . .

FELICITY. I'd be absolutely helpless without her, I'd never be in time for a single meal. My hair would be all over the place and I should be covered in safety pins from head to foot.

MIRANDA (*crossing to* R *of Felicity*) Now look here, Lady Marshwood, I think we'd better come to an understanding about this.

FELICITY (*moving to the chair down* L) By all means. (*She sits*) What do you suggest?

MIRANDA (*crossing to* L *of Felicity*) I suggest that Dora should be given a nice little cottage somewhere or other and a reasonable pension. I haven't discussed this with Nigel, but I'm sure he'd agree. . . .

FELICITY. I've no doubt he would, but you see he doesn't depend on her to do his hair every morning and I do.

MIRANDA. I admit that I haven't behaved very well to Dora, and I'm sorry for it. I'm willing to try to make it up to her in any way that I can.

FELICITY. You said just now that you never intended to speak to her again until the end of your days.

MIRANDA. I know I did, and I'm sorry for that, too. (*She crosses below the sofa to the fireplace*) I haven't slept a wink all night and my nerves are on edge. (*She leans against the mantelpiece*)

FELICITY. Would you like some Phensic? I have some in my room. Moxie knows where it is.

MIRANDA (*gazing into the fireplace*) No, thank you.

FELICITY. We're all feeling a little jaded this morning. Nigel, of course, did the most sensible thing. He went galloping off across country, but we couldn't all do that because there aren't enough horses. As a matter of fact I believe May has a bicycle that she isn't using at the moment.

MIRANDA (*turning*) You don't want me to marry Nigel, do you?

FELICITY. Not at the moment, Miranda, but I am sure I shall get used to it. I'm very adaptable. I expect we shall both have to make certain allowances just at first, but we shall doubtless jog along together all right after a while.

MIRANDA. Jog along together?

FELICITY. I know it doesn't sound very alluring put like that, but you do know what I mean, don't you?

MIRANDA (*moving down* R) I do. I'm not quite as stupid as you think.

FELICITY. I'm so glad.

MIRANDA (*moving below the sofa*) I also know that you planned all that business of Dora dressing up, just to belittle me in front of Nigel, just to make me look a fool.

FELICITY. I had no idea that you yourself would contribute so generously to the final result.

MIRANDA. Then you did?

FELICITY (*rising*) No, as a matter of fact, I didn't. (*She moves down* C) The whole thing was improvised, foolishly I admit, to spare Moxie's feelings and your feelings, temporarily at least.

MIRANDA (*sitting in the chair* R) Do you expect me to believe that?

FELICITY. You can believe it or not as you like, but it happens to be true. Of course I knew that the fact of you and Moxie being sisters was bound to come out eventually, but I hoped by that time that you and I would have got to know each other well enough, and like each other well enough to discuss the situation rationally and calmly. (*She moves down* L) Unhappily it didn't turn out like that.

MIRANDA. It most certainly didn't.

FELICITY. Moxie, enraged by your imaginative flights, lost her head and gave the game away, and I must say I can't blame her. (*She crosses and stands below the sofa*)

MIRANDA. You may not blame her, but I do.

FELICITY. The only thing you can possibly blame her for is not dying of drink.

MIRANDA (*rising and crossing to* R *of Felicity; beginning to lose her temper*) Well, I'll tell you here and now. Before I set foot in this house as Nigel's wife, she's going to be out of it for good.

FELICITY. On the contrary, she will receive you at the front door. We might even prevail upon her to drop you a curtsy. The press photographers would love it.

MIRANDA. You forget one thing. Nigel happens to be in love with me. He won't stand by and allow me to be publicly humiliated.

FELICITY. Are you so sure?

MIRANDA. What do you mean by that?

FELICITY. Nigel is my son, Miranda, and, like his father before him, he has one ingrained temperamental defect. He loathes disharmony, detests scenes and runs like a stag at the first sign of a domestic crisis.

MIRANDA. Are you trying to suggest that owing to all this—this business of Dora being your maid, that he won't marry me?

FELICITY. Certainly not. Nigel is a man of his word. I am merely giving you a word of warning.

MIRANDA (*crossing to the fireplace*) I don't need any warning, thank you.

FELICITY (*moving to the desk*) Really, Miranda, for a successful and world-famous woman you are quite remarkably silly. (*She collects the menu*)

MIRANDA. How dare you speak to me like that!

FELICITY. You forget, my dear, that I am already, virtually, your mother-in-law. (*She crosses above the sofa*) And as it seems fairly obvious that we are destined to have an endless series of unpleasant scenes during the next few years, I think we might curtail this one now, don't you? (*She moves to the hall door and turns*) We usually leave for church just before eleven.

(FELICITY *exits to the hall, closing the door behind her.* MIRANDA, *clenching and unclenching her hands, moves to the hall door then turns and crosses quickly to the french windows.*

NIGEL *enters from the hall. He now wears a lounge suit*)

Nigel (*crossing to Miranda*) Miranda! I thought you were still asleep.

Miranda (*turning*) Still asleep! I haven't closed my eyes all night.

Nigel. Darling—I'm so sorry.

Miranda. I'm going away, now, this morning. I'm catching the eleven-fifteen from Deal.

Nigel. You can't possibly.

Miranda. And why not I should like to know?

Nigel. It's an awful train. You'll have to change twice. Ashford and Maidstone.

Miranda. Your mother has insulted me.

Nigel. I'm sure she didn't mean to. You really mustn't take mother seriously. She just rattles on, you know, she doesn't mean half she says.

Miranda. She says she's going to live in this house—with us. Is that true?

Nigel. Of course it is. She's always lived here.

Miranda. Nigel!

Nigel. Now do calm down, darling.

(Miranda *crosses above Nigel and stands above the sofa*)

You won't have to see much of her, except in the evenings. She has a tremendous amount to do during the day. She runs the whole place, and the village, too. She's on God knows how many committees. She's practically an institution.

Miranda (*taking a green handkerchief from her bag*) Do you expect me to sacrifice my whole life, my career, everything—(*she points to the hall doors*) to live with an institution?

Nigel. I never asked you to sacrifice anything. You said in Cannes that you were weary and lonely and wanted to get away from it all, and that all your fame and success was a hollow mockery. You even burst into tears when that poor young man tried to take a snapshot of you outside the *Palm Beach Casino*.

Miranda (*crossing to* R *of Nigel*) Your mother hates me. Don't you understand? She hates me.

Nigel. Nonsense! You're imagining things. She's probably a bit irritable this morning. After all, the scene last night was upsetting; the house is under-staffed with one maid ill and the other away——

(Miranda *crosses below Nigel and sits in the chair down* L)

—and she's got the church fête on Friday. She has a lot to try her.

Miranda. *She* has a lot to try her? What about me?

Nigel (*moving to* R *of her*) Now look here, Miranda . . .

Miranda (*turning her back to him; near to tears*) You don't love me. That's clear enough at any rate. You never came near me last night.

NIGEL. You slammed the door in my face.

MIRANDA. And this morning, without a word of sympathy or understanding, you went out horse-back riding. (*She weeps*)

NIGEL (*moving below the left end of the sofa*) We just say "riding" in England. The horse-back is taken for granted.

MIRANDA. I'm not going to live in this house with your mother. And that's final.

NIGEL (*crossing to* R *of her; icily*) As my wife, Miranda, I shall expect you to live where I live and do what I ask you to do, and the first thing I ask you to do here and now, is to make every effort to be on good terms with my mother. I loathe and detest family scenes and what is more I have no intention of putting up with them. (*He moves slowly above the sofa to the hall door*) I am quite sure that at the first sign of a gesture from you, Mother would be prepared to meet you more than half-way. (*He stands in the open doorway*) And I can see no earthly reason, with good will on both sides, why you shouldn't jog along perfectly happily together.

(NIGEL *exits to the hall with great dignity and closes the door behind him.* MIRANDA *rises, gives an inarticulate cry of rage, then crosses to the sofa, sits on it and weeps.*

After a few moments, DON *enters from the hall, closing the door behind him*)

DON. Pete!

MIRANDA. Go away.

DON (*moving slowly down* R) Don't cry. You know it always ties me up in knots to see you cry.

MIRANDA. I can't bear any more—I can't.

DON. What's happened, kid? Has that stuffed shirt said something to upset you?

MIRANDA (*controlling herself with an effort*) No, Don, it's nothing. Please go away. I shall be all right in a minute.

DON (*crossing and sitting* L *of Miranda on the sofa*) How can I go away and leave you—like this?

MIRANDA. You must, Don—you really must. (*She touches his hand*) There isn't anything you can do. (*She rises and crosses down* C) This is my problem and I've got to grapple with it alone.

DON. If that high-hat English louse said anything to make you cry I'll poke him in the nose.

MIRANDA (*turning to him*) No, Don, don't do that—it wouldn't do any good.

DON (*rising and moving to* R *of her*) Why were you crying?

MIRANDA (*gallantly*) A moment of weakness, that's all. I just felt suddenly lonely and sort of bewildered.

DON (*unhappily*) Oh, Pete.

Miranda (*dramatically*) Life can be very cruel sometimes, Don. It can do terrible things to people—(*she crosses to the downstage pillar of the alcove and drapes herself against it, facing down* L) especially to over-sensitive, trusting fools like me.

Don. You're no fool, Pete. You're smart as a whip—you always have been—you're a fighter, too—(*he crosses to* R *of her*) that's one of the things I love best about you. You've got guts.

Miranda (*turning*) Thanks, Don—Pete.

Don. You're not going to let this—this bunch of café society bit-players give you the run-around, are you? You! Miranda Frayle. You must be out of your mind.

Miranda. What's the use of talking, Pete? (*She turns her back to him*) Maybe I am out of my mind. Maybe I have made a mess of things, but I can't walk out now. I've signed the contract.

Don. You walked out of *Dreams Cannot Lie* after they'd been shooting for two weeks, contract or no contract. Where's your spirit? Why they even suspended you for three months and you laughed in their faces. At least they can't suspend you here.

Miranda. They can do worse than that. They can torture me and humiliate me. They can—(*she turns; falteringly*) they can break my heart.

Don (*enfolding her in his arms*) Not while I'm around they can't. I'm the guy that loves you—remember?

Miranda (*emotionally*) Oh, Pete!

(Don *and* Miranda *passionately embrace.*

Felicity *and* Nigel *enter from the hall. They are dressed for church.* Peter *follows them on and stands in the doorway.* Nigel *stands above the right end of the sofa*)

Felicity (*moving down* R) Really, Miranda. This is becoming monotonous.

Miranda (*disengaging herself from Don's embrace*) I feel that you and I have nothing further to say to each other, Lady Marshwood.

Felicity. I'm afraid that will make our long winter evenings together rather insipid. (*To Peter*) It looks as though we shall have to have a television set after all.

(Peter *moves down* R *and stands above Felicity*)

Nigel (*crossing to* L *of the sofa; with dignity*) What does this mean, Miranda?

Miranda (*with dignity*) It means that I am going away.

Nigel. I know you are. You said so a little while ago. I'll drive you up after lunch. You can't possibly go by train.

Miranda. Don is going to drive me up, before lunch. Aren't you, Don?

Don (*crossing below Miranda to* L) You bet I am.

FELICITY. Well, we really can't stand about here arguing as to who drives who. We shall be late for church.

(CRESTWELL *enters from the hall*)

CRESTWELL. Mr Don Lucas's car is at the door, Milady.

DON (*delighted*) O.K. Come on, Pete. (*He crosses above Miranda and Nigel to the hall door*)

NIGEL. I would rather you didn't drive to London with Mr Lucas, Miranda.

DON (*moving between Nigel and Miranda; threateningly*) You can just quit ordering her about from now on, see? She's coming with me—now! Get it?

FELICITY. Please don't be belligerent, Don. You're not rescuing anybody from the Japanese now, you know.

DON (*crossing to Felicity*) I'm sorry, Felicity. But she's coming with me, right away. She's not going to stay here and be tortured and humiliated any more. (*He moves above the sofa*)

PETER (*to Felicity*) You see he *does* think we're the Japanese. It's a sort of occupational neurosis. (*He moves to the fireplace*)

NIGEL. Miranda. You insist on leaving with Mr Lucas?

(CRESTWELL *picks up Miranda's raincoat from the chair up* R)

MIRANDA. Yes, I do. I couldn't stay here. I couldn't live in this house, not with things as they are. (*She gives Felicity a venomous look, crosses to Crestwell and takes her coat from him*) I was a fool ever to think that I could. (*She puts on her raincoat*) I'm walking out on you, Nigel. I'm sorry, but that's how it is. (*She crosses to the hall door*) And you can tell my sister from me that she can go on doing your mother's hair for as long as she has any to do. Come on, Don.

(MIRANDA *exits majestically to the hall.* DON *gives an embarrassed look at Felicity and follows Miranda off*)

FELICITY (*handing her handbag to Peter*) Poor Miranda. (*She puts on her gloves*) She's been on edge all the morning.

NIGEL (*moving down* LC) This is all your doing, Mother. I hope you're satisfied. You engineered the whole thing. You deliberately drove her into the arms of that lout.

FELICITY (*crossing to Nigel*) I did not. She's been in and out of his arms like a Jack-in-a-box ever since he set foot in the house.

NIGEL. You've behaved abominably, and I'm ashamed of you.

FELICITY. And I am most bitterly ashamed of you. You, a Peer of the Realm and a member of *White's*, allowing the woman you love to be whisked away from under your nose without a protest. I can hardly believe it. (*She crosses to Peter, and takes her handbag from him*)

NIGEL. Of all the hypocritical nonsense. You wanted to get rid of Miranda and you succeeded. You're absolutely delighted.

FELICITY (*crossing to Nigel*) And you? Are you going to stand there and pretend that you're heart-broken? You seem to forget that I'm your mother, dear. I brought you into the world, in the middle of Ascot week, and I know you through and through. You never really loved Miranda, any more than you really loved any of the others. Of course I'm delighted. We're all delighted. And now for Heaven's sake let's go—(*she moves above the left end of the sofa*) we're terribly late, the last bell went ages ago.

(MOXIE *enters from the hall. She wears her hat and coat*)

Ah, there you are, Moxie. I couldn't think what had happened to you.

MOXIE (*moving above the sofa*) I've come to say good-bye, Milady.

FELICITY (*crossing to* L *of Moxie*) Rubbish! Take off your hat and don't be silly. (*She searches in her handbag*)

MOXIE. But, Milady . . .

FELICITY. Do as I tell you, and for Heaven's sake someone give me some money for the collection. There's nothing more to worry about. I haven't time to go on about it now, but Crestwell will explain. Come along, everybody. Crestwell, give Moxie a glass of sherry, she looks as if she's going to fall down. Come, Nigel, it's your first Sunday at home and you must try to look as though nothing had happened. After all, when you analyse it, nothing much has, has it? Peter—we shall have to go by the footpath because of all those Girl Guides.

(FELICITY *crosses and exits by the french windows.* PETER *crosses and follows her off.* MOXIE *crosses to the alcove.* NIGEL *is about to exit when he suddenly sees Moxie's expression*)

NIGEL (*moving to* L *of Moxie*) Cheer up, Moxie. Everything's all right now.

(NIGEL *pats Moxie on the shoulder then turns and exits by the french window*)

MOXIE (*tremulously*) Thank you, my lord. Thank you ever so much. (*She crosses to the sofa, sits on it at the left end, and rummages in her bag for her handkerchief*)

CRESTWELL (*crossing and standing above the left end of the sofa*) Snap out of it now, Dora. You heard what he said.

MOXIE. It's all very fine for you. You haven't made a public exhibition of yourself and cried your eyes out all night long.

CRESTWELL (*crossing to the table down* L) Even supposing I had, I should have the sense to shut up now.

MOXIE. You haven't had the ground suddenly cut from under your feet and been shamed and humiliated by your own flesh and blood. I'll never be able to hold my head up again and that's a fact.

CRESTWELL (*pouring two glasses of sherry; cheerfully*) In that case we shall have to settle for it hanging down, shan't we? (*He crosses to* L *of the sofa and hands Moxie a glass of sherry*) Here—away with melancholy—have a swig of this.

MOXIE (*dimly*) Thanks, Fred.

CRESTWELL (*crossing and standing below the right end of the sofa*) As I see the situation, Dora, you've got hold of the wrong end of the stick. You're not the one that's been shamed and humiliated. It's the other way round. Your only mistake, if I may be permitted to venture a slight criticism, is, that you didn't take the golden opportunity when you had it, to give your own flesh and blood a nice healthy slap in the chops.

MOXIE (*with a slight giggle*) Oh, Fred.

CRESTWELL (*raising his glass*) I give you a toast, Dora. I drink solemnly to you and me in our humble, but on the whole, honourable calling. I drink to her ladyship and his lordship, groaning beneath the weight of privilege, but managing to keep their peckers up all the same. Above all I drink to the final inglorious disintegration of the most unlikely dream that ever troubled the foolish heart of man—Social Equality. (*He drinks*)

MOXIE (*removing her hat and fussing with her hair*) No-one's ever going to stop you talking, are they? (*She drinks*)

CRESTWELL. It would, I admit, be a Herculean task, but should you feel disposed to have a whack at it, you have only to say the word.

MOXIE. That'll be the day and no mistake. (*She giggles*)

CRESTWELL. What about another nip at the Amontillado?

MOXIE. I don't mind if I do.

The CURTAIN *falls for the first time. When it rises again* CRESTWELL *crosses to the table down* L, *picks up the decanter and crosses to Moxie as—*

the CURTAIN *falls*

FURNITURE AND PROPERTY PLOT

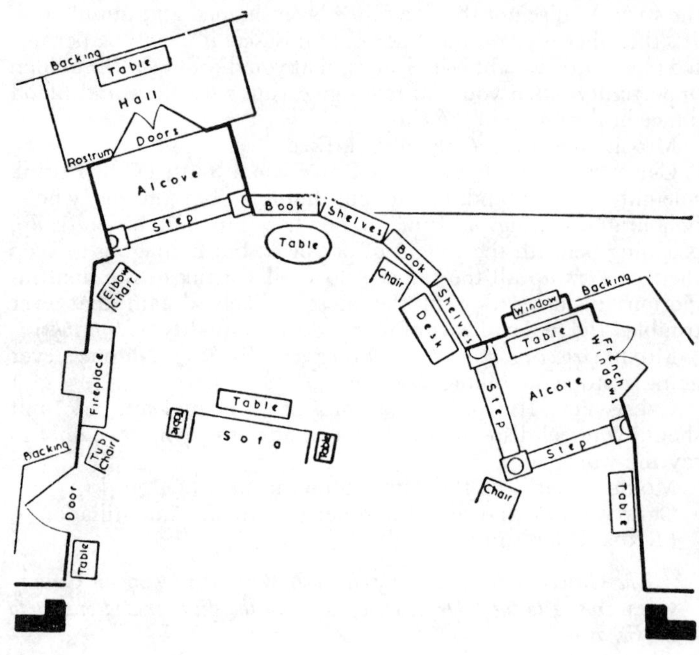

ACT I

On stage: Games table. *On it:* ornament, ashtray
Tub chair. *On it:* cushion
Occasional table. *On it:* ornaments
On mantelpiece: vases, ashtray, table-lighter, matches, box with cigarettes
Fender
Fire-irons
Large brass jug with leaves as firescreen
Elbow chair (*up* R). *On it:* cushion
Built-in bookcases. *In them:* books
Oval table (*up* C). *On it:* books, table-lamp, magazines, ashtray, table radio, bowl of roses
Desk chair
Waste-paper basket

Desk. *On it:* inkstand, pens, pencils, blotter, table-lamp, ornaments, rack with stationery, ashtray, books
Alcove table. *On it:* ornaments, ashtray, vase with flowers, work-box
Table (*down* L). *On it:* tray, decanters of whisky and sherry, bottles of gin, lemon squash and vermouth, soda syphon in stand, glasses, table-lamp, ashtray
Elbow chair (*down* L)
Sofa. *On it:* cushions
Table (L *of sofa*). *On it:* box with cigarettes, lighter, ashtray, small vase of flowers, magazines
Table (R *of sofa*). *On it:* ornaments, ashtray, box with cigarettes
Table (*above sofa*). *On it:* telephone, newspapers, copy of *The Times*, magazines, box with cigarettes, matches, ashtray

Pictures on walls
Carpet on floor
Rug at fireplace
Rug below sofa
Rug in alcove
2 electric wall-brackets
Bell-lever below fireplace
In hall: runner
table. *On it:* ornament
picture on wall

Scene 1

Set: *In desk drawer:* fête list, fête map
On desk: 2 used cocktail glasses
On table down L: used cocktail glass
On mantelpiece: used cocktail glass
On table L *of sofa:* Felicity's spectacles, used cocktail glass
On sofa at left end: Felicity's handbag
On table up C: used cocktail glass
Rumple cushions on sofa
Double doors open
French windows half open

Off stage: Tray (Crestwell)
Dustpan (Alice)

Personal: Moxie: handkerchief
Lady Hayling: watch

SCENE 2

Strike: Felicity's handbag

Set: Small circular table below right end of sofa. *On it:* tray, pot of tea, jug with milk, basin with sugar, 2 each cups, saucers, spoons, plate of sandwiches
Tidy cushions
Double doors closed

Personal: PETER: case with cigarettes, lighter

ACT II

SCENE 1

Strike: *The Times* from desk

Move: Lighter from mantelpiece to table R of sofa
Felicity's spectacles to desk

Set: *On table down* L: 8 cocktail glasses
On sofa: knitting
Tidy cushions
Double doors closed
French windows open

Off stage: Tray. *On it:* cocktail shaker, long spoon, container with lemon peel (CRESTWELL)
Ice bucket with ice and tongs (ALICE)

Personal: MIRANDA: work bag. *In it:* needlework, spectacles
MOXIE: spectacles, handbag. *In it:* handkerchief

SCENE 2

Strike: Everything from table L of sofa except 1 cocktail glass
Miranda's work bag
Cocktail shaker and spoon
Tidy cushions
Double doors open

Off stage: Tray. *On it:* pot with coffee, basin with sugar, jug with milk, 8 each coffee cups, saucers and spoons (CRESTWELL)

Personal: DON: cigarettes, lighter, 20-dollar bill
PETER: cigarettes, lighter
MOXIE: handbag

ACT III

Strike: Moxie's handbag
Coffee tray
Dirty cups
Dirty glasses
Ice bucket and tongs

Set: *On sofa:* copy of *The Observer*
Re-set table L of sofa. *On it:* vase of flowers, box with cigarettes, lighter, ashtray
On table down L: 2 sherry glasses

Off stage: Tray. *On it:* glass of brandy and ginger ale, saucer with 3 aspirin (CRESTWELL)
Tray. *On it:* autograph books (CRESTWELL)

Double doors open
French windows open

Personal: DON: handkerchief
MIRANDA: raincoat, handbag. *In it:* green handkerchief
FELICITY: handbag, gloves
MOXIE: handbag. *In it:* handkerchief

LIGHTING PLOT

Property fittings required:
    2 electric wall brackets (practical)
    3 table lamps (practical)
Interior. The same scene throughout
The Main Acting Areas are RC, C, and LC

ACT I SCENE 1
    Afternoon
    The apparent sources of light are the windows in the alcove L

To open: bright sunlight

No cues

SCENE 2
    Afternoon

To open: bright sunlight

No cues

ACT II SCENE 1
    Early evening

To open: sunset

No cues

SCENE 2
    Late evening

To open: twilight outside windows
    wall brackets lit
    table lamps lit

No cues

ACT III
    Morning

To open: sunlight

No cues